Copyright © 2016 by Melodieann Whiteley

All rights reserved. No part of this publication may be reproduced, distributed, or transmitted in any form or by any means, including photocopying, recording, or other electronic or mechanical methods, without the prior written permission of the publisher, except in the case of brief quotations embodied in critical reviews and certain other noncommercial uses permitted by copyright law. For permission requests, write to the publisher, addressed "Attention: Permissions Coordinator," at

info@beyondpublishing.net

Quantity sales special discounts are available on quantity purchases by corporations, associations, and others. For details, contact the publisher at the address above.

Orders by U.S. trade bookstores and wholesalers. Please contactBeyondPublishing.net

First Beyond Publishing soft cover edition April 2016

The Beyond Publishing Speakers Bureau can bring authors to your live event. For more information or to book an event contact the Beyond Publishing Speakers Bureau atspeak@BeyondPublishing.net

The Author can be reached directly at MelodieannWhiteley.com

Manufactured and printed in the United States of America distributed globally by Beyond Publishing partners

New York | Los Angeles | London | Sydney

10 9 8 7 6 5 4 3 2 1

ISBN 978-0-9961486-6-5

Forward

I recently was invited to a dinner where 10 out of 25 people had earned over $1,000,000 in the last year. It was at an internet marketing conference and we were all there to learn, grow, and connect and meet new people. Yes some were there to sell things, but the majority of these people understand the magic. That magic that got them there in the first place. That magic that would keep them there. That magic that made them viable, accessible, and relevant! If you want: Knowledge, Perspective, and Insight…You've come to the right place. But let's start by answering these three tough questions. What do you want? How will you get there? Who will help you?

What do you want?

So you want to own your own business? You want to be in control of your own destiny? Is that why you join a network marketing company? That is what most people expect: growing earnings, growing returns on initial time investment, and getting paid by finding others to sell what you sell for you and your up manager.

You picked up this book or audio book because you are involved in network marketing somehow, some way. You have a desire to learn from those who have been there, done that and become successful doing NM or MLM.

We all don't know what we don't know. Is this going to be worth your time? Well that is up to you! Some of us have all the answers (I was not invited to that club). I call myself a professional student, because I have hit that point where life slapped me upside the head and said…"HEY STUPID… You have so much more to learn."

Now, I can call myself STUPID because I have been there, done that, and learned from my mistakes (sometimes more than once). Seriously, when you stop learning, you have shut down. You are smarter than everyone else. You have so much experience, that people climb mountains to hear your wisdom. You become a deity.

No one, including you and I, is beyond learning

How will you get there?

So let me give you the shortcut that will take you from where you are to sitting at the table with (or becoming) one of those $1,000,000 earners that everyone else wants to have dinner with.

Let me start by telling you what every one of these people had, and that I learned that night. The key to success is not just looking out for number 1… It's often more important to think about number 2,3,4,5 and so on who become your best understudies or customers. You have to focus on the success of others in order to obtain true success. If you are only in it for yourself, sooner or later people will figure it out and disengage

You cannot buy success when your reputation is in the 1/2 off bin at Wal-Mart.

You don't get there by treating people like a prey. You get there by realizing that people are people. They want to learn and be as successful as you. The cool thing that I have learned is that the smart people don't have unlimited time to make you successful, but they will invest in people who are smart and can pay it forward to other people.

Those millionaires (and everyone else at that dinner table) realize that by paying it forward, it comes back in ways that you could never have imagined before achieving success. It just pays off and they don't ask how or why... it just does. It's not so much about "What Can You Do For Me"; it's more about "What Can I Do For You" (in small and measured bursts). They just do what they do because they love what they do, and they care about other people and want them to become successful based on their knowledge and efforts.

It's spending time to plant a seed. Farmers plant dozens, thousands, and even millions of seeds. Not everyone bears plants or fruit. Have you ever seen a farmer go back to where they planted and say "What the heck happened?" No... they focus and nurture the plants that grow and forget about the seeds that refuse to blossom.

The way that you get there...is to nurture positive relationships. Embrace the ones that grow, and ignore the ones that refuse to blossom!

Who will help you?

EVERYONE…but not who you think. Network marketing logic says to start selling to those who are closest to you. That is what works. Those are the people who KNOW, LIKE, and TRUST you. They are easy prey.

Please don't do that.

Start by getting to know people first, and then ask them how you can help them. Get to know their needs and wants. Get to know how you can help them solve their problems. Give to them without any expectations and watch what happens…

Help others first, then watch and wait. If you have the GREATEST product since SILLY PUTTY, no one cares because they are trying to protect themselves from being taken advantage of. They may look at you as someone who is trying to separate them from their money.
If you do sell them in the short run, that can do more damage in the long run.

START CARING! If your product or service can really help people, spend time, invest time, but more importantly, teach, train, inform, and give – expecting nothing in return. The best customer is the one that sings your praises because you solved their issue, or filled a gap, or made their life better.

Who will help you? Your evangelists who help you convince others to stop and take a look at
what you have to offer.

Why This Book?

Melodieann is a friend and living proof of the fact that when someone likes and believes in your product or service they become a huge asset for your business. She is a successful entrepreneur who is still there and doing that. Your business and life will benefit so much from her insights, wisdom and experience. Trust me…it is so much better having a cheerleader talking with you than a critic.

If you want to learn from someone who has "Been There, Done that," you have come to the right place. You will learn WHAT is important, HOW most of what you hear from MLM trainers and veterans is outdated, and WHO you really need to communicate with and follow to obtain sustained success. That is WHY you are reading this book, right?

In this book, you will learn how to do it right! You will get insightful knowledge from someone who has been there and done that. It's about paying it forward and getting the most from someone who wants you to succeed.

Most importantly, it's about how YOU can pay it forward to ensure your own success. This book will show you how to open your mind to becoming a successful Network Marketing consultant, trainer and advocate. If you think it's all about building more drones below you in the MLM chain to sell your stuff…please drop this book and go back to your day job.

If you are ready to learn…sit back, grab a notebook, and be prepared to be amazed!

Written by Brian Basilico

Table of Contents

Introduction 10
Chapter 1   Overcoming Network Marketing Fears 14
Chapter 2   How To Effectively Handle Any Objection 18
Chapter 3   Is This One Of Those Pyramid Things? 22
Chapter 4   Why Network Marketing? 25
Chapter 5   I'm Not Sure I'm Cut Out To Run My Own Business... 32
Chapter 6   What Will People Say? 35
Chapter 7   I Can't Sell 40
Chapter 8   I Don't Know If I Can Recruit People 42
Chapter 9   I Don't Know Anything About Online Business 51
Chapter 10 I Can't Afford It Right Now 53
Chapter 11 There's No Guarantee 58
Chapter 12 How Can I Find The Time? 64
Chapter 13 I've Tried "These" Before... 70
Chapter 14 There Are So Many Opportunities Just Like This One...73
Chapter 15 I Need To Ask My Spouse 75
Chapter 16 All My Friends Told Me This Will Never Work! 78
Chapter 17 Understanding Personal Attraction 82
Conclusion 88
Appendix 90

Getting To Yes

OVERCOMING
NETWORK MARKETING
OBJECTIONS

6/8/2014

Melodieann Whiteley

Introduction

ARE YOU READY TO QUIT? WHY YOU SHOULDN'T!

I meet someone who is looking for a way to make some extra income. I talk to them, get to know them, build a trusting relationship with them. I know in my heart that I can help them. And they seem receptive. They want what I have. I can see it in their eyes, hear it in their voice. They like me. They trust me. We are both excited about the possibilities ahead. And then…the objection bomb falls.

Network marketing? Are you crazy?

Aren't those illegal?

No one makes any money with network marketing. Everyone knows it's just a rip off!

That's just a scam!

These are just a few of the reactions I have gotten when presenting my business opportunity to prospects. And although it doesn't happen often, I admit that when it does, it can be frustrating and discouraging. And it's worse when it comes from a family member or friend. They KNOW what you do. They have seen that it works. They should know

I care about their well-being and want to see them succeed. And yet the objections come. It's like being slapped in the face.

So why do it anyway?

Meet Linda Gracy. Twenty-five years ago, she was teaching high school math. She loved it, at least until her daughter was born. But once she became a mom, those maternal hormones kicked in, and it just killed her to have to go off and leave her daughter every day. Then when her son came along, it was even worse. In the morning, when it was time to head off to school, her kids would lock their arms around her leg and hang on. Linda says, "It would tear my heart out of my body to have to pry their little fingers off, and to walk to the car with both of them crying and my daughter saying 'Mommy, don't go!' There were days I actually cried half the way to school! The day the nanny excitedly told me that she had witnessed my son's first steps, it absolutely broke my heart! I decided right then that there HAD to be a way, in this great land of America, that a mother could stay home and raise her own kids! That's when I started searching for a way to make money working from home."

Linda HAD to find something that would replace her teaching salary if she was going to be able to quit her job and stay home with her preschoolers. Network marketing was the only thing she could find that would do that. Then she stayed in network marketing because she knew that she could never make enough money with just her own efforts to support the lifestyle she wanted for herself and her family. There is obviously a limit to how much money you can make in almost any traditional career. But with network marketing, there is no limit because you leverage your time. If you have a team of 100 people, for example, and they each put in 5 hours, you get paid on 505 hours of work instead of just the 5 that you put in yourself. The bigger your team grows, the more hours you get paid for.

I keep doing what I'm doing for people like Linda, and everyone else looking for an opportunity. Almost anyone can be successful in network marketing. All it takes is time and perseverance.

I know the question that comes next. "If network marketing is so wonderful, how come more people aren't actually making money at it?" Because too many team leaders still teach their downline team members to build their business by chasing after every warm body they can find. First you hound your friends and family until they no longer speak to you. Then you buy leads and start calling. And you know what you get for your troubles? A lot of objections from everyone you talk to. This is not how to succeed in network marketing. It's all about relationships. If you are going to immediately drown everyone you know in what you do and how it can help them, you might as well give up now. No wonder your family avoids you. I wouldn't want to be around you either!

But it is possible to overcome all those objections. And in the process, build your team without harassing everyone you know. How? That's the purpose of this book.

Overcoming Objections

No matter how great your website is, or how inspiring your personal story, prospects will always have objections. Learning how to effectively deal with them and teaching that skill to your team members will be the key to your network marketing success. This book will address some of the most common – and not so common! – myths and objections to network marketing I have heard in my years of experience in this business. The techniques I use to deal with them will help you overcome these network marketing objections. I know they work, not only because I have used them successfully and taught my team to use them, but I learned them from some of the best network marketers in the business. You can modify them to suit your particular needs, but this advice will give you the basic information to get started.

At the end of each chapter, there will be action steps to implement, recommended resources to help you, or in-depth tips and techniques to try. If you truly want to be successful, then practice these steps even if you haven't encountered any objections yet. Being prepared when the moment comes will increase the likelihood that you will get past the objections and go on to enroll your prospect.

I'm Here to Help You

I will do everything I can to help you succeed. As a baby boomer, I know what it's like to wonder if you will be able to retire one day. I've watched my husband worry how he would support us as his health declined. I know how my dad worried about being a burden to me and my family. You'll read my story later in the book. I understand the stress money worries can cause, and I want to help you succeed in your own network marketing business.

I will do everything I can to help you succeed. Don't believe me? When you purchase this book, connect with me through the business email address listed on my website and I'll send you my personal email address. Feel free to contact me anytime. And if I can't answer your question, I'll try to find someone who can.

Are you ready? Take the first step now. Turn to Chapter 1 and learn the key to overcoming network marketing fears.

Let's do this!

Chapter 1

OVERCOMING NETWORK MARKETING FEARS

I was so excited! My company was having a promotion. If I could hit my sales quota or add a new member to my downline, I could win a free cruise! And I was almost there. My team and I had sold more product this month than ever, and I had a hot prospect ready to join my team. She was excited about the possibilities. I had talked to her on the phone the night before and she was ready. "Call me tomorrow night and we'll do the paperwork so I can get started." I was already packing for my trip as I dialed her number. And then – the dreaded objection. I couldn't believe what I was hearing.

"I'm not sure I like having to make a minimum purchase each month. And I'm not sure about recruiting others. I can sell without any trouble, but I'm not sure I can get other people to join my team."

Wait a minute! We had already discussed this. What happened? What had I done wrong? I tried mightily to persuade her that everything was fine. She would be great. Our team would help her build her downline. The minimum purchase was not a problem. The products were so fantastic that I regularly purchased far more than the minimum. But nothing I said mattered. I finally hung up, dejected and dismayed. I had gone from planning a Caribbean cruise to facing a cold and dismal winter at home. I wish I had known then what I know now. I would have been on that cruise ship, soaking up some Caribbean sunshine!

One problem seems to cause more objections to a network marketing business than any others.

Fear.

Part of Network Marketing is networking. The other part is marketing. Both of those involve getting your message in front of people. Both of these can be fun. But for many would-be network marketers it's the worst thing in the world.

Meeting strangers? Trying to convince people we've never met – or even worse, people we know well! - that network marketing is a legitimate business model and this opportunity is for real? Picking up the phone to follow-up with a prospective customer or business partner? What if they laugh at me? What if they say no? What if they tell me I'm going to ruin my credibility by being associated with this business? (That actually happened to a team member of mine.) And of course we all know that it takes a special kind of person to be successful in business. If this was so simple, everyone would be doing it. Besides, I'm too old, too busy, and too poor to start a business now.

I had to face many of these fears myself when I started. It may be hard to believe now, but I used to be painfully shy. Talking to strangers? Why, just the thought made me ill. Even if I could somehow get up the nerve to make a presentation, why would they listen to me? I wasn't anyone special. I had actually grown up fairly poor. Surely they would be able to tell what a phony I was. And then they would laugh at me for pretending to be a successful business person. I was so paralyzed by my fear that I couldn't show my products or my business opportunity to anyone except my family. And they weren't interested because, just as I had expected, they knew me all too well and knew that I was just a fraud.

I finally gave up on the whole idea of network marketing. Everyone was right. It didn't work for people like me.

Fast forward twenty years. My life today is so different. I make a good living doing something I love. I am a successful entrepreneur. What happened to make it all possible? After all I am still the same person I was the first time I tried this. And I was busier than ever when I started the second time. I was working a full-time job and caring for my dad who had Alzheimer's disease. I had grandchildren. A husband and home to care for. So what changed? My motivation. It's amazing what you can accomplish when you have the right motivation. And I had a colossal need to be able to stay at home.

I had a dad who needed full-time care and no money for a decent nursing home. I had daughters with children of their own that couldn't find decent, affordable childcare. I NEEDED to be able to stay home. I also needed to be able to earn a living. It's amazing what you can do when you have no other choice. Because I desperately needed this to work, this time I took the time to actually learn how to make it work. I learned to overcome my fears. And I learned to help others do the same.

Your prospects are afraid of some or all of these same things. But rather than admit their fear to you, they will come up with one objection after another. For the most part, these horrors of being judged, rejected and ridiculed are just imagination. I'm not saying some of your prospects won't be ridiculed. They will. And yes, some of your prospects will hear several "no's." That's okay. It's a matter of helping your prospect to identify their "why" so that their true motivation can carry them through the scary parts and on to the parts that are golden and make it all worth their while.

Action step:

The fear is real. But it can be overcome. Here are three action steps you can take to help your prospects move past their fears.

1. Learn all you can about your business. Understand the compensation plan. Know how the products work. Be able to explain why you are so passionate about them and the company. Know what training is available and how to access that training.

2. Get to know those who are successful within your industry. Use your upline team members to provide validation until you are making money yourself. Learn from them. They obviously know what it takes. Talk to them and discover what steps, techniques, marketing methods, and prospecting tips they have to share.

3. Be confident about your opportunity and let your prospects know that you have confidence in their ability to be successful. Confidence is contagious. If you don't have faith in yourself and your business, why would anyone else? And if you don't show your prospect that you believe in them, why would they believe in themselves?

4. Listen to the particular objections your prospect is making. Often that will give a clue to what their underlying fear really is. Then, instead of addressing that particular objection, address the fear.

Chapter 2

HOW TO EFFECTIVELY HANDLE ANY OBJECTION

If you are in network marketing, or any business, you will receive objections from prospective team members and customers. Learning to handle them effectively can determine whether you sponsor a prospect or not. For instance, the "pyramid scheme" is an objection I hear all the time. I didn't know how to answer it until I discovered this quote – and the answer to the pyramid objection.

"I am often asked if Network Marketing is a Pyramid Scheme. My reply is that corporations really are pyramid schemes. A corporation has only one person at the top, generally the CEO, and everyone else below." – Donald Trump

I love Donald Trump's response to the question of pyramid schemes. I admit I never thought of corporations that way until I read this quote. But he is right. I used to work for a major corporation. At the top was the president of the company. Below him were several vice presidents. Below each of them were several directors. And below each of them were several department managers, who each had several department supervisors below them. And finally below the supervisors were hundreds of regular employees. No matter how hard I worked, I would never make as much as the president, or the vice presidents, or the directors, managers, or even the supervisors. I might eventually get promoted to supervisor, but only if a supervisor also got promoted or left and created an opening. But in network marketing I can go as high as I want, and without having to wait for the person above me to leave an opening.

So, now I have a thorough answer to the objection, and can even pull from my own experience. Learning to handle objections effectively is critical to your business success. Often the way a prospect responds to you will depend on how you respond to their objections. If you are evasive or defensive, don't have an answer to their questions, or try to minimize their concerns instead of addressing them, all you are doing is reinforcing their fears that somehow network marketing is wrong. I had to learn this lesson the hard way through trial and error. Fortunately, you get to learn from my mistakes.

There are tips and techniques for handling specific objections. However, there are some basic rules that apply no matter what the objection is. Use them and you will be able to handle any objection a prospect throws at you.

The Rules

The rules I'm going to share should be universally applied to all objections, including the ones listed here in this book. They will serve as a foundation for the advice I'm going to give you, but should also be mastered as a technique you apply to all objections. That way, even when you run into an objection that isn't covered here, you'll be ready to face it head on.

Listen! Let them ask their question or voice their objection completely before you respond. It's important that you really hear what they are saying. And while you are listening to the words, also listen to tone and inflection. Observe body language. Often the objection they are voicing is not the real problem at all. If you can determine that and answer the underlying issue, you have won a new recruit. These people are looking for what you have. If you don't listen to them and give them a voice, they will find someone who will.

Confirm that you heard what was said. This may require you to repeat/reflect what is being said and ask questions. You can do this by paraphrasing what was said and then asking questions to clarify. "What I'm hearing is…." "Is this what you mean?" Or you can repeat the objection or question exactly as stated by your prospect to confirm that you were listening.

Validate their concerns without giving approval of the objection. Show that you understand their objections and then ask how you can make them feel more comfortable and at ease. Handle the objection. Now that your prospect knows that you have heard his concerns and are genuinely interested in trying to help him, he will be much more receptive to what you have to say. Now is the time to address the specific objection using the tips given for each. Remember, most objections are really indications of an underlying fear. Handle the objection, and probe for the fear that is the root. Then address the fear.

The Scripts

Now that I've given you universal rules you can apply to any objection, you may be wondering, "So why bother discussing specific objections at all?" The reason is because the advice and examples I give you next will serve you like a script. Once you've become intimately familiar with the most likely and common excuses people will give you, you will be prepared to address them when they come up – even before they come!

This will allow you to adeptly address the issue and move on. Yes, I still want you to sincerely listen; no, I don't want you to give a canned response. But running through these unique scenarios now will save you from having to reinvent the wheel later, or giving your prospect the worse response of all – "I don't know."

I'm sure you're familiar with the phrase, "Hindsight is 20-20." Unfortunately, it's usually after you've given the wrong response (or a wide variety of wrong ones) that you realize what you should have said. My aim is to help eliminate that learning curve for you so you can get right down to doing what you've set out to do – earn money and change lives.

And so, without further ado, let's move on to the most common myths and objections in our industry, and solutions for how to address them.

ACTION STEP:

If you do not have good listening and communication skills, now is the time to strengthen them. Take training in effective listening and communication. Check the Resources section of this book for recommendations on courses or coaches.

Chapter 3

IS THIS ONE OF THOSE PYRAMID THINGS?

One of the first questions I inevitably get when presenting my business opportunity is, "Is this a pyramid scheme? Aren't those illegal?"

I know that pyramid schemes and scams exist. I was once part of a company that was eventually shut down by the FTC for that reason. When I started, they were an excellent company. But as they became more successful, they began to change. The product line was changing. There were fewer actual marketable products being added. And many of the ones we did have were discontinued. Our training calls became less focused on product information and more focused on recruitment methods. Fortunately, I did not like the direction they were taking, and neither did many of my team, both upline and downline. We all left the company before they became a full-fledged rip off. And we were not surprised to hear a few years later that they had been closed by the government. I won't name them here, for legal reasons, but those of you who know what company I was with several years ago know which one I am talking about!

Let me state once and for all – network marketing is not a pyramid scheme. Pyramids do exist and sometimes it's hard to tell a legitimate business from a scam. Being able to explain the difference will help overcome this objection. But how do you tell the difference?

Network Marketing Opportunities vs. Pyramid Schemes

1. A legitimate network marketing business will have a genuine product or service. This product or service will have value of its own and be priced accordingly. In a pyramid, there is usually no real product or service. If there are products or services, they are often greatly overpriced.

2. A legitimate network marketing business will disclose any information about the company to anyone interested in knowing more. Pyramids offer little to no information about the company unless a prospect purchases the products and becomes a participant.

3. Network marketing businesses encourage the sale of the products or services offered by the company. Commission is paid on these sales to reps involved in the business. Pyramids promote an income stream that chiefly depends on the commissions earned by enrolling new members or the purchase by members of products for their own use rather than sales to customers who are not participants in the scheme. Focusing on enrolling new members over obtaining new customers is a huge warning that this could be a scam.

4. n a network marketing company, the money to pay commissions comes from the sale of products or services. In a pyramid, the money to pay commissions comes primarily from the participants buying products for their own use or by enrolling new members.

5. In a network marketing company, you can earn a decent living. In a pyramid, 90% of the participants never recover their initial

investment. Since there are no real products, there is nothing to sell to make money. And once you run out of people to recruit, you stop earning signup bonuses. That is if the company doesn't fold first because it isn't adding new recruits fast enough to keep up with the promised payouts.

6. In network marketing, your income is based on how hard you work. You can advance as high as you wish and earn whatever you want. In a pyramid scheme, those at the bottom can never advance higher or make more than those at the top.

Pyramid schemes do exist. They get more sophisticated and harder to spot all the time. But there are many good, solid, legitimate network marketing companies also (see "The Top 10 Network Marketing Companies" in the Appendix). If your prospects are looking for a way to make some extra income, or even one day replace their job with a business of their own, they are ready for what you have to offer. But you must be able to calm their nervousness about being scammed or doing something illegal by explaining why network marketing is not a pyramid scheme. If your prospect asks this question, now is not the time to continue to pitch your business. Focus on educating them instead.

Action Step:

Know the difference between a legitimate network marketing business and a pyramid scheme. Review the differences until you are able to explain them clearly and concisely to your prospects. Rehearse if you must. Enlist the aid of family and friends to listen and critique you.

Chapter 4

WHY NETWORK MARKETING?

"Network marketing is not a real business. Why would I want to get involved with it?" This is one of my favorite objections. Someone is looking for an inexpensive way to start a part-time business. They think network marketing may fit the bill. But they are afraid it may be too good to be real. It's your job to show them the many benefits of having a network marketing business.

There are hundreds of reasons to join a network marketing business. You have been downsized and can't find a new job. You would like to retire but can't afford to. Your health won't allow you to continue in your current job and you don't know what else to do. You would like to spend more time with your children. You have to replace the income of an ailing spouse. Or maybe you're just tired of working all day for someone half your age that makes 3 times what you do.

Or maybe you are like Alice Burke. When I met Alice, she was a single mother of four with a high school education and no prospects. When I introduced her to network marketing, she grabbed onto it with everything she had. She saw, for the first time in years, the possibility of a good life for her and her children. She borrowed the money for the enrollment fee, signed up, and went to work. When she started, she was always one step ahead of the bill collectors, juggling and pinching pennies to make ends meet. Today, she and her children live in a nice home, drive a new car, and don't have to decide between rent and electricity, food or school clothes. As she told me, "My oldest daughter wanted a laptop computer since she starts high school this year. You don't know how satisfying it was to be able to get her one. It may not sound like much to some people, but when you remember that a few years ago, you were struggling just to put food on the table, it's a miracle!"

Whatever your reason for starting your own business, the number one reason to try network marketing is this – IT WORKS!

Why network marketing?

When David Letterman asked Donald Trump what he would do if he had to start over, the answer amazed me. He said, "I would find a good network marketing company and get to work." Now, you may not like his politics or some of his actions, but you have to admit one thing; Donald Trump knows how to make money.

Many other famous entrepreneurs like Warren Buffett, and Rich Dad Poor Dad author Robert Kiyosaki are either directly involved in network marketing businesses themselves or recommend it to their followers. And if it's good enough for Donald and Warren and Robert, it's good enough for me.

Many recognizable brand names – Tupperware, Mary Kay Cosmetics, Avon, Melaleuca, Ariix, Pampered Chef, Thirty-One – fall under the network marketing umbrella. Some of these companies have been in business for years. Melaleuca has been in business for 29 years. And what woman hasn't tried or at least heard of Avon? And my own mother was a Tupperware representative. She didn't stick with it very long, but right next door to us was a woman who put 3 kids through college as a Tupperware representative.

These types of programs feature a low upfront investment – usually only a few hundred dollars for the purchase of a product sample kit–and the opportunity to sell a product line directly to the people you know. Most network marketing programs will also ask you to recruit sales reps who will become your downline. As their recruiter, you're entitled to earn commissions on their sales as well.

There are many benefits to having a network marketing business.

1. You can own your own business relatively inexpensively. Some of us may be lucky enough to have accumulated some savings that could be used for a business investment, but many baby boomers are facing retirement with barely enough to live on and certainly don't want to risk it on a business. The cost to start a network marketing business is usually small enough that you can own your own business without tapping into your savings or borrowing money. There is no upfront investment needed for a location or fancy equipment. All you pay is a startup fee for your starter kit. A network marketing business can be started for anywhere from $50 - $2000, depending on the company you choose (see "How do I know which Network Marketing Company is best?" in the Appendix). I have seen start-up fees as low as $30. Try to buy a McDonald's franchise for that!

2. You can work at your own pace. Many network marketers start part time and stay at their regular jobs while they build their business. Once they have built their businesses to the desired level, many quit to pursue their business full time. Others choose to only work it part time to bring in some additional income. Either way, you

get to make a choice.

3. The power of leverage. You will hear us talk about leverage in our business presentations and training. In a traditional business, you are paid only on the number of sales you make or customers you see. In network marketing, you can build a team of people who also own their businesses. Then you get paid on your own sales AND you receive a percentage of sales from all of your team members. I get paid for the work of hundreds of team members.

> Let me explain how leverage works. I have a friend who works for a car dealership. He does fairly well - as long as he works "bell to bell" (open to close) 5-6 days a week. He sells on average 15-20 cars per month. But if he goes on vacation or is ill, he sells nothing and makes nothing. Now, suppose that he had a team of other salespeople that worked for the same company. He recruited them, trained them, and supported them, and in return he received a percentage of their sales. If he had 10 salespeople on his team and they each sold 5 cars apiece each month, that's an additional 50 cars a month that he receives some money for. Plus he still sells his 15-20 per month. If he gets sick or takes a day off, he might not sell his 20. But he will still get paid his share of the additional 50.
>
> Now let's take it one step further and say each of these 10 salespeople were allowed to do the same thing. They each recruited 10 members for the team and everyone got a percentage of the sales. So now my friend has another 50 (10x5 = 50) sales he gets a percentage of. Plus the 50 from the team he recruited. Plus his 15-20 each month. That's potential sales of 120 cars – all with no more time or effort than it took to sell his 15-20. THAT'S called LEVERAGE!
>
> Another form of leverage is the system that is already in place

for you. If you join a network marketing program, everything is already in place for you. All you have to do is learn from those that have gone before you and been successful and copy what they did. No need to start from scratch.

4. A growing market. Do you know anyone with a cell phone? Satellite TV? Do you know anyone who takes vitamins or uses weight loss products? How about cosmetics? Do you know anyone who travels? Shops at Target, Barnes and Noble, KMart, or other stores online? Needs a home security system? Is interested in Identity Theft Protection? Has long distance on their home phone? Has considered Vonage or another VOIP company? These are all potential customers and there are network marketing companies that offer all of these products or services. Do you know people that would be interested in making a little extra money in their spare time or would like to learn how to build financial security? These are all potential business partners.

5. Unlimited income potential. In network marketing you can earn as much or as little as you want. It all depends on how much time and effort you are willing to put into the business. My husband and I decided to work like crazy for 3-5 years. We did so because we fully intended to be at a position financially at that point that we could retire. Some of our team members are already making more than we do because they worked the business full time from the first day. There is no one to tell you how much you earn per hour. There are no salary caps. And you can earn promotions whenever you want to based on how hard you are willing to work.

6. Location. You don't have to worry about location. Most network marketing businesses are run from home. I started mine in my bedroom. Or you can use the kitchen table, a corner of the dining room - even some space in the garage. I have a team member who still works a job and so has just started part time. Since his

job requires him to travel frequently, he has turned his car into a mobile office and works out of it when not on the job.

7. Home business tax deductions. There are many things you can deduct once you own your own home business. And who couldn't use a few more tax deductions? For example, this year I was able to claim some of my gasoline (for driving to business meetings and presentations), some meals (customer and prospect dinners), part of my internet costs (I use the internet for my business), part of my cell phone costs (ditto), some of my travel costs (by combining our vacation in Orlando with a business seminar, part of my trip was deductible). Of course you really must consult with a CPA or other tax professional to ensure you follow all the IRS guidelines. And by the way, the CPA is deductible.

8. Residual income. Even when my husband and I retire, we will still earn income from the team members we have recruited that are still working - and still recruiting additional team members.

9. Ease of entry. You don't need any special skills to get started. Network marketing is one of the few businesses that train you as you work. All good network marketing teams hold regular training sessions to help new members build solid business.

10. Time! Time for your family, time for yourself. In a network marketing business, you can work as much or as little as you please. It all depends on how quickly you want to build your business. And you can take the time you want off. I was able to attend my grandson's kindergarten graduation. In my old 9-5 job, I would have had to miss it. I would not have been able to get the time from work to attend and I normally wouldn't have left the office until 8:00pm. But now that I have my own business, I simply planned my day so I was free in time to see him in his first little cap and gown. How cute! I have a friend who was not hired

for a job simply because his Sabbath is Saturday and the company insists that everyone work on Saturday. When my friend stated he could not work Saturday, he was not hired. (I know – there is some questionable legality here.) He recently joined my team and now his Saturdays are his own. He gladly works Sunday on his business and has Saturday to spend with his family and God.

> Time also means you can take all the time you need to build your business. In the corporate world, I watched many co-workers come and then go when they weren't able to meet a quota. In network marketing, the only quotas are the ones you set for yourself. On our team and on most teams in general, if you are willing to work, we will work with you no matter how long it takes.

Is Network Marketing For You?

Becoming an entrepreneur is not for everyone. There are risks involved in any business and questions to answer before starting any venture. Are you ready to start a business? How much money do you need to make? How much can you afford to invest? Your choice of companies may be affected by how much you can spend to get started. Most companies have reasonable enrollment fees but there are some that can be expensive.

Are you physically able to do the work? Network marketing is one of the easiest businesses to work, but I am a Boomer. I am closing in on 60 fairly quickly. I may have a few more aches and pains, move a bit more slowly, see a bit less clearly, not hear as well as I used to. My fingers may stiffen up when I type too long. Having some physical limitations doesn't mean you can't be successful in this business. It just means you may have to take a different approach.

What is your exit strategy? At our age, that is a definite consideration. Some companies will let you include your business as part of your inheritance. If not, what happens to the team you built when you are gone?

Do you have the skills necessary? As I stated earlier, there really aren't any "special" skills required. Yes, basic computer skills are helpful. And the ability to talk to people doesn't hurt. But more important than skills is passion and desire. We can teach you the skills. If you have the drive and determination to succeed, all you really need is the ability to build relationships with people.

Action Step:

Network marketing is a real, legitimate business opportunity. Be able to explain the benefits of owning a business, especially a network marketing business. Again, practice is key, so rehearse, rehearse, rehearse until you can list the benefits quickly and clearly.

Chapter 5

I'M NOT SURE I'M CUT OUT TO RUN MY OWN BUSINESS

Becoming an entrepreneur can be frightening to someone who has never before considered the possibility. Yes, it can be extremely rewarding. But there are always risks involved in any business venture. They are minimal in network marketing, but they are there.

What do you do when you hear this objection? Have an honest conversation with your prospect. The key is to find out if they really are unsure of their business skills or if they are just frightened of the unknown and using this as an easy objection.

When I hear this, the first thing I do is ask to show the business to the remaining family members (spouse, older children, parents). If the family is supportive, often this can provide your prospect with enough confidence to move forward. And if they are not, you will know right away that it is unlikely this prospect will be successful.

If the family presentation goes well but your prospect is still hesitant, this is the time for an in-depth conversation. The goal is to help them determine for themselves, with your guidance, whether they are ready to be an entrepreneur. Unfortunately, not everyone is, no matter how wonderful your business opportunity is.

Use the following questions to get an honest conversation started that will help you both determine whether they are a good fit for your opportunity. The more "yeses" your prospect says, the more likely they will eventually say yes to your opportunity, so try to phrase the questions in such a way to elicit that response. For example, instead of asking someone if they are self-motivating, I may ask them if they require a lot of supervision at work. When they say "no", I ask "so you are able to get your daily tasks done on your own?" And the answer is invariably, "yes."

1. Are you self-motivating?

2. Do you manage your time effectively?

3. Are you willing to take some risks?

4. Do you communicate effectively?

5. Are you ready to set goals and create a plan to reach them?

6. Do you have the financial means to pay the enrollment fee?

7. Can you manage your finances wisely?

8. Can you promote yourself and your business using the methods we will teach you?

9. Are you healthy enough to put in the hours and do the work?

10. Are you teachable?

11. Are you organized?

If your prospect doesn't answer yes to most of these, then you may want to rethink bringing them onto your team. It does take most of these to be successful. Starting a business isn't for everyone.

However, if they are only lacking a few of these, then congratulations! You may have a new team member. The skills and traits they have can significantly contribute to their success. And they may be able to learn or acquire what they lack with coaching and training.

ACTION STEPS:

Try to get the prospect's support team on board by presenting the opportunity to their friends and family.

Help your prospect assess their skills and determine if they are ready to become a business owner.

Chapter 6

WHAT WILL PEOPLE SAY?

Even though we can effectively prove that network marketing is a legitimate, profitable business opportunity, there are still people who believe that network marketing is hard, bad, unethical, sleazy, slimy, manipulative, dishonest and doesn't work. So what? There are people who say the same thing about insurance salespeople, lawyers, car salespeople, and politicians. And yet I'll bet you have insurance and a car and have used or considered using a lawyer.

But for every person that thinks this is a slimy business, I can give you an example of someone that has made it work and changed lives. David who was able to quit his full-time job and work half as many hours; Pam who jumped in with both feet and was out selling me in a matter of months; Ernie who supports himself and his disabled wife. And then there are the top dogs – names that we've all heard. Robert Allen, Tim Sales, Mike Dillard.

There are many voices and opinions about this business, just as there are about everything. It's up to you to decide which ones you're going to listen to.

"Network marketing gives people the opportunity, with very low risk and very low financial commitment, to build their own income-generating asset and acquire great wealth." - Robert Kiyosaki

"The future of network marketing is unlimited. There's no end in sight. It will continue to grow, because better people are getting into it. They are raising the entire standard of MLM to the point where soon, it will be one of the most respected business methods in the world." -Brian Tracy

If you listen to all of the naysayers, they will have you believe that every network marketing business in the world is just another opportunity for you to lose your money. And yet there are hundreds of people making a decent living every day with Avon, Mary Kay, Pampered Chef, Ariix, Melaleuca, and Herbalife - just to name a few. What? These are not all network marketing business opportunities? Of course they are. Any business that rewards you for building a team underneath you is network marketing.

Why do people have such a negative view of our business? It could be any one of several reasons. Perhaps they have been approached before by someone who really didn't understand the business. Or perhaps they were approached before by someone who was only interested in adding one more person to his team and so behaved inappropriately. It might not have anything to do with network marketing at all. Your prospect might look at all home-based businesses as being some sort of scam. It's very likely they have tried it and failed. And once that happens they are convinced it's because they are all scams. They fail to realize that it's like any other business. You will get out of it what you put into it. How many people did they show the business plan to? One? Two? Then someone laughed at them, or they got tired of hearing no, and they became embarrassed to admit they were in network marketing, and they quit. How many people did they show the products to? I'll bet they were even less enthusiastic about that. They came into the business thinking they were just going to build this tremendous downline and not have to sell any of the products.

Maybe they have been involved in network marketing previously but weren't really taught how to build a business and so didn't make the income they were expecting. Perhaps they were even told they would make hundreds of thousands of dollars within a few months. Will all network marketers become wealthy? No. But then you are not going to become wealthy doing what you are already doing either. If you were, you would be rich by now!

Network marketing has created more millionaires than any other business. Can you say that about your job? And what if you do not get rich? Is that so necessary? I got started in my business so I could have some spare income. Housing prices are on the rise again. Food prices are climbing higher every day. Jobs can still be hard to find. If you could make an extra $800 - $1000 every month, would that help? Of course it would.

The secret to success is simple: Once you sign up, get to work. Don't worry about the naysayers. If they can't see the benefits of your opportunity, thank them for their time, show them your products and ask if they will become a customer, ask them for a referral to someone who might be interested in either your business or your products, then say "NEXT" and move on. Don't try to bully them into joining, don't keep bothering them once they've said no - just thank them for their time and move on to your next prospect.

The best way to show people that network marketing is real is to become successful yourself. How do I recruit people now? When they ask me what I'm doing for a living, I tell them. When they comment on the fact that it's only May and my husband and I have had two vacations already this year, I tell them how we pay for that. When a friend laughingly said she wished she could have money like I have so she could eat out as often as my husband and I do, I tell her how we are able to afford to. And then they either get it or they don't. If they do - excellent! Sign 'em up! If not, they never will. NEXT!

Tips and techniques:

- Be sure of yourself and what you have to offer. Confidence is attractive. People who are poised and self-assured just naturally draw others to them.
- Make a list of all the skills and qualities you have that will help you be successful as a network marketer.
- Know all the benefits of owning a home business.
- Be sure you can explain why network marketing is the perfect home business for most people.

Your beliefs impact everything you do. If you doubt yourself or your business, your prospects will pick up on that and will be hesitant to join your team. You need to be totally confident in yourself, your company, your products, and your ability to be successful.

Chapter 7

I CAN'T SELL

Great! Because if you think you are going to make a ton of money in network marketing by just selling the products, you're in the wrong business. Network marketing is not about sales. It's about building a team and coaching them to success. Remember the concept of leverage? Not only do you get paid for your own efforts but also for the work of your entire team. That's why it's beneficial to you to help every member of your team become as successful as possible.

Now don't get me wrong. You do need to sell the products. Where do you think the money comes from to pay your commissions? And your team members will also have to sell some products. (If someone tells you that you don't have to sell anything, watch out. They either expect you to buy a lot of it yourself, or it's a scam or a pyramid).

The beauty of network marketing is that you can combine some sales work with lots of coaching and team-building work and generate a very nice income. For example, when I started my business, I immediately became my own customer. My nutritional supplements, my skin care products, my cleaning products, my weight loss program - all these are now purchased through my businesses. Then I went to people I knew already used the products and services that we offer and asked them if they would purchase them from me. Since I wasn't asking them to buy anything they weren't already paying for, most of them said yes. So I started out with six customers. Then I started building my team and coaching them to do the same. Soon I had a team of 300 people. So with some beginning sales work I started earning a small commission. Then with some coaching and team-building, I built a strong team and taught them to do the same thing I did. So, assuming that each of my team members has the same six customers I started with (some actually had more), I would receive commission on 1800 customers, not including my own. And in the course of building my team, I picked up some additional customers.

I built this team in a little over 2 years. How long do you think it would have taken me to find over 1800 customers on my own? Quite a while. That's the beauty of network marketing. My direct sponsors each went out and sponsored some people of their own, who sponsored some of their own, who sponsored some more...and on and on until I have hundreds of team members and thousands of customers.

Selling isn't the most important skill in building a successful network marketing business. Coaching and team building are far more critical skills. If you aren't strong in those two areas, I'd suggest you start learning. Because that's what will make your business grow. Check the Resource section of the book for tools to help.

ACTION STEP:

If your coaching and team building skills aren't strong, immediately start getting the training you need to strengthen them. Make a list of 5 books and 2 mentors you can utilize to help. You can also reference the Resource section of this book for more tools.

Chapter 8

I DON'T KNOW IF I CAN RECRUIT PEOPLE

The key ingredient to a successful network marketing business obviously is a good team. While it is possible to make money just by selling the products produced by your company, the fastest way to success is to build a team of like-minded business partners. Since you receive a percentage of everything they sell as well as the profit from your own sales, you can see how this quickly adds up. My team consists of almost 500 business partners, which makes a huge difference in my income each month.

However, many people I talk to are easily sold on the merits of this business opportunity, but aren't confident that they can share their passion in a way to interest others. They are afraid that they won't be able to recruit anyone into their downline and really master the power of leverage. This is usually because they don't think they have anyone to share the opportunity with, or because they think they are going to have to immediately go out and call their closest friends and family members and try to convert them. I will now show you how to easily overcome this fear.

I Don't Know Anyone To Show This To

When I was in the Navy, two things accompanied me on every move. We never went anywhere without my books and my music. In fact, we have been known to pay excess shipping costs just so I could move them from duty station to duty station.

These things are still extremely important to me, but two things have replaced them as my most prized possessions. My Rolodex and my laptop. Okay, I don't actually have a Rolodex anymore. But I do still have a contact list and it's one of my most important possessions.

I don't care what business you are in, you can't succeed without people. Whether it's your clients, associates, competitors, employees - people are the lifeblood of your business. This is especially true in network marketing. And the simple truth is you know more people than you realize. Sit down right now and start making a list. Everyone you know. Your hairdresser. Your children's teacher. Their coach. Their Scout leader. Your mailman and newspaper carrier. Your neighbors. The woman behind the counter at your favorite store. Your insurance salesman. Your car salesman. Your doctor. The list goes on and on. See – you already have quite an extensive network!

Your network should be a prized possession - one that is cultivated and nurtured carefully. Your network will provide you with an ongoing supply of people to do business with, ask advice from, collaborate with, mastermind with, and seek assistance from to help your business grow and prosper. My Rolodex contained all the business cards I'd collected in the course of my daily interactions with others. Today, instead of placing cards in a Rolodex, I enter the information into my contact management program. And with my laptop I can connect with almost anyone I know, anytime, anywhere.

Cold Feet with the Warm Leads

If you've been in network marketing before or are currently involved with a company, then you know that most organizations encourage you to recruit what they call your "warm market" first. That's your family and friends.

This may sound like a good idea. This is familiar turf with people who hopefully already know, like and trust you. However, it often just doesn't work that way. These people know you. If you have struggled to make ends meet for years, your credibility will be lacking when you try to convince family that you have a profitable business opportunity. If you have a history of starting more things than you finish, it may be difficult to convince your friends to join a team that may not be there tomorrow. You may even be rejected because of your success. Family and friends who don't know how you are suddenly surpassing them and are afraid to try may reject and ridicule you because they are jealous and can't admit they are afraid to reach for what you have found.

While I'm not saying that friends and family can't make good recruits, I encourage my team members to look at other methods. Friends and family can be a tough sell. They know you and they may want to wait and see how successful you are before they climb on board. Or, if you have been like me, and tried many companies before finding the right one, they may think this is just another of your latest "schemes" and that, as usual, you will drop out as soon as it gets tough.

Advertise and Market

If you don't pursue friends and family, how do you find prospects? That's easy. Start treating your business like a business. What do other businesses do to attract customers? Advertise and market. Start advertising and marketing your network marketing business and you will attract qualified and interested prospects - without hounding everyone you know personally.

The key words here are "attract interested prospects" and "without hounding." This is known as "permission based marketing." Permission based marketing means you only communicate marketing materials to people who have given you permission to do so. This mostly refers to email marketing, but it can also apply to telemarketing, mailers, or just about any form of marketing communication. Consumers are constantly being barraged with marketing messages. Consequently, they have learned to tune out what they don't want to hear. Admit it. You have a junk email address. It's the address you give when you have to provide an email address but really aren't interested in further information from the company. If you persist in marketing to people who have not given you permission to do so, at best your message will just be ignored. At worst, you will get a reputation as a "spammer." If people are not answering the phone when you call, not responding to your voicemails, or – heaven forbid! – crossing the street when they see you coming so they can avoid talking to you, you definitely need to familiarize yourself with this concept.

Website

How do you get your message out to your prospects? The first thing you need to do to start marketing is to have a website. Yes, most companies have websites they provide. Some of them are actually pretty good. The problem is it's the same website all 100,000 reps in your company are using. You need something different that will set you apart from the rest of the crowd. It can be as simple as a blog. It doesn't have to be fancy. You just need a place to put your presentation online, provide a way for prospects to contact you, capture the contact information of those who may want additional information, and follow up with them. Having your presentation online makes it available for viewing anytime someone wants, 24/7. It means you can have unlimited viewing instead of being constrained by how many people can fit into your living room for a DVD presentation. It allows people to contact you anytime, night or day, whether you are immediately available or not. And if you have an autoresponder, it follows up with your prospects automatically. More and more companies are encouraging their members to have websites, as long as you adhere to their guidelines, so be sure you know what they are and follow them. There are several simple tools available to build your website. I have listed these in the Resources section of this book.

Be the Expert

Next, you need to know all there is to know about your business. People want to do business with leaders. Experts attract others wanting information. If you can't answer their questions, they may not come back a second time. If you have to go to your sponsor every time I ask a question, why don't I just save time and go to your sponsor myself? Make sure you know:

- How the compensation plan works
- What the products are
- How promotions to the next level are earned
- What training is provided by the company
- What marketing materials are available to prospective team members

The Law Of Duplication

Learn how to market your business effectively and teach this to your team members. If your company holds any type of training, be sure you participate. Skip the weekly "Rah-Rah" meetings, unless you really enjoy them, and learn how to master online marketing and prospecting. Use conference calls and teleseminars to teach these skills to others on your team. Word will quickly spread that your team is the one to join because you know how to attract and train great people. Once you master these skills and then teach your team to duplicate them, you'll be amazed at how quickly your business grows.

Once you master these skills, your business will be easier, more fun, and will duplicate faster and better than any team that's solely dependent on the old methods of in-home meetings, cold calls, and buying leads.

Networking

Networking does not mean attending every event and passing out your business card to every warm body in the room. It does not mean joining every social networking site you can find, posting your information, and waiting for clients and business partners to come calling.

If you really want to be an effective networker, you must participate. When attending networking events, when you give someone your business card use this tip I learned from one of my mentors. Write on the back of it these 4 letters - HCIH. HCIH - How Can I Help. Instead of introducing yourself and launching into a lengthy explanation of what you do, give a brief explanation. Then ask them about their business. And then ask how you can help. Often they will actually tell you. Sometimes they won't. Either way, let them know that you may be able to help them and promise to send them some information that may be helpful. I keep several reports and articles always updated so I have the information ready. Then as soon as I get home, I email or mail them the pertinent information. I have now established two things with them - my value and my commitment to helping them succeed.

Social Media

Twitter, Facebook, LinkedIn, Google+, Instagram, Pinterest. Social media networking is a fabulous tool to engage with prospects. Through the different social media platforms, you can meet and interact with prospects from all over the world. It's a great way to build relationships with prospective business partners and customers. Social media allows you to interact in different ways. You can gain new customers by teaching them about your products and how they can benefit their lives.

Share business insights and advice to position yourself as the expert in your field. People like to associate with experts and will want to follow you.

Interact with others. Answer questions. Give advice. Look for those who are searching for what you have to offer and watch for the opportunity to make it available to them.

When using the various social networking sites, don't be a "lurker." Share your knowledge by posting articles and advice for others to share. The best way to show people how much you can help is by demonstrating your willingness and ability to do so.

You also can't ignore your contact list until you need something from them. Check in with everyone on the list periodically. Ask how they are doing. Ask how you can help. Treat them to lunch or coffee. Send them a card or a short note or an article you read that might interest them. Show them you care. People like working with people they know and trust. What better way to build that trust than to show them that you care about their success. Comment on their social media posts. Retweet, Like, Pin, and Share!

In the old days, home parties, buying leads, and cold calling were the methods used to find customers and team members. And in some circumstances, they still work. But when you learn to harness the power of the Internet and master the art of attracting customers and team members to you (this is known as attraction marketing), you will become unstoppable!

Action Steps:

- When a prospect tells you they don't know anyone, help them prepare a list of contacts to show them just how large their network actually is.
- Invite team members and prospects to networking events and show them how to effectively use these to make connections. Set up your social media sites and begin interacting with other members.
- Help prospects and team members set up social media pages if they don't already have them. If they do, then encourage them to connect with you and show them how to use social media correctly to build relationships.
- Become familiar with your company's guidelines for online marketing and websites. Determine if you are permitted to build your own or if you must use one provided by the company exclusively.
- Set up your website, lead capture page, and autoresponders, if available.
- Learn all you can about your business. Know the products and how they work. Use the products! How can you recommend

something you don't use yourself? Understand how the comp plan works, especially how and when team members get paid and what it takes to move to the next level. (See "Network Marketing Compensation Plans" in the Appendix.)

- Prepare your presentation. Just because you are prospecting online does not mean you will never have to give a business presentation.
- Practice your presentation until it is smooth and professional. Have friends and family listen and provide input. Who knows? You might even recruit a couple of them.
- Choose one or two marketing methods to try each month and implement them. Note which work for you and add them to your regular marketing arsenal.

Chapter 9

I DON'T KNOW ANYTHING ABOUT ONLINE BUSINESS

If your prospect is a member of my generation, this could actually be an honest objection. They may be a bit technology-challenged. I know it took me a while to learn the difference between a blog and a website, what a URL was, or how to host a teleseminar. Sometimes it's a bit embarrassing to admit my grandchildren are as comfortable with the computers as I am. Even the 6-year olds are pretty computer savvy! But hey! I didn't grow up with computers everywhere like they did

It is possible to build a successful network marketing business without the use of online marketing techniques. But it is much harder and will take substantially longer. You do want to encourage your team to use all of the tools at their disposal and that includes the internet. It increases their chances of success dramatically. That is one reason my team teaches everyone how to market their business online.

ACTION STEP:

Assess your prospects general computer skills. If they are comfortable enough with a computer to use basic programs like browsers and email, assure them that is enough to get started and they can learn the rest as needed.

Show them the online tools available to them that don't require a great deal of skill. If your company has a replicated website for representatives, demonstrate how it works. If you host online webinars, show how easy it is to invite someone.

Show them the resource section of this book. Many of the tools listed are designed to simplify the online marketing process. Assure them that when they are ready to move forward, you will show them how to use these tools. Or you can do what I do - give all your new reps a copy of this book.

Chapter 10

I CAN'T AFFORD IT RIGHT NOW

Yay! I just added another person to my team! For a minute or two, I wasn't sure it was going to happen. He got a little concerned when I told him what it was going to cost to get started. He thought that was a lot to pay for a business of his own. It made me stop and really question whether he even really needed to be on my team. After all, if the cost is your first consideration, perhaps you aren't ready to own a business. Yes, cost is important, but my first question was, "How much can I make?" not, "How much is it going to cost?"

Before my team member was able to sign up, we had to work on his mindset. You will occasionally find people that will never be financially secure, no matter how much money they make. Their mindset is not one of prosperity but of lack. Until they take responsibility for their situation and learn to change how they think about themselves and money, they will never be successful. You do not want these people on your team. They will be discouraged because they are not successful and they can spread that feeling to other team members. Lend them this book and direct them to the chapter on attraction marketing (chapter 17). They will either get it or they won't. If they do, you will know fairly quickly. Sign them up. If they don't, know that there is nothing else you can do and walk away.

But for those who literally can't find the padding in to their budget to pay for this, it's up to you to help them see things a little differently so they can find it. I guarantee if anyone who thinks our fee is too much will just take a look at what they spend each month, they will discover they spend that and more on things that do nothing to improve their future. How do I know? One $4 latte every day, rain or shine, at Starbucks, added up to $120 of my spending every month. Add the $2.50 muffin to that and it was $195 a month. And 360 cable channels, over half of which we never watched, added up to $70 a month. That's $265 a month! Cut out all this unnecessary spending. That's how I paid for my enrollment!

So how did my newest team member pay for his?

Well, first there was that newspaper subscription he never read. And there was the gym membership he had - which he also never used. And then there was....

An Investment

You may be wincing at the idea of cutting out some of these so called luxuries from your life, but let's look at this realistically. You are investing money in your future. For that you receive the right to do business as a representative of our company. You receive all of your marketing materials, order forms and enrollment forms. You receive the weekly rep support email from corporate, access to tons of conference and training calls, and the ability to market some truly remarkable products. You receive the benefit of our team's years of success. You get the combined experience of some of the top moneymakers in network marketing. You don't have to stock any inventory. You don't have to worry about billing and collections. You don't have to repeatedly make sales calls and take orders and then make deliveries. And most importantly, you get me and my team. Let's be blunt. If you make money, we all make money, so you can be assured we will do all we can to teach you how to be successful in this business.

I asked some friends of mine who are all business owners what it cost them to start their ventures. Are you ready?

    The Business Broker: $16,000

    The Event Planner: $7,000

    The Day Care Center Owner: $33,000

    The Computer Expert: $550

    The Caterer: $1,100

    The Pizzeria Owner: $65,000

    The Personal Trainer: $2,700

    The Doggie Day Care Owner: $25,000

    The Personal Shopper: $2,500

    The Landscaper: $5,000

    The Housekeeper: $500

    The Florist: $75,000

    The Café Owner: $88,000

The average start-up, based on these figures, costs $24,719. That's a lot of money! Most of these women started their businesses a few years ago, so with the economy the way it is right now, I'm sure the costs would be higher. And they don't receive the added benefit of having everything provided for them. Nor do they have a team dedicated to helping them succeed.

What it costs to start a business is one of the things you need to think about when considering stepping out on your own. And sometimes the enrollment fee for a network marketing business is not a small amount of money. But it's not just about the cost of the business. It's about the value of the investment.

Tips and Techniques:

When a prospect tells you they can't afford it, help them look at the unnecessary spending in their budget. If they cut it out, remove it from their normal spending, often it will be enough to cover their enrollment costs.

Many companies have "Quick Start" bonuses. If your company does, share how these can often help new enrollees earn their initial investment back quickly, often within the first month or two.

If that still does not work, then encourage your prospect to find ways to save up or acquire the money in some other fashion. I do not encourage borrowing the money. Unless you are absolutely certain your prospect is going to work the business and be successful, it is not good to encourage new enrollees to start out by going into debt.

I have occasionally paid the enrollment fee for a new team member. Some companies allow this and some do not. Be sure you follow the guidelines for your company. If you decide to take this step, be sure you and your new team member are clear on the arrangement. I have done it several different ways.

1. Almost every opportunity has different "levels" of entry that come with varying amounts of the company's products. If I am paying for a team member to come in at one of the higher levels, I will sometimes take part of the product from their initial shipment and sell it to recover my investment.

2. Several team members have wanted to keep all of their product and have agreed to simply pay back the loan. I do draw up an agreement in this case, more for their peace of mind than mine. I don't charge interest in these cases, and having that in writing puts new team members at ease.

3. There have been a couple of times when I knew in my heart that a prospect simply was not going to be able to ever come up with the enrollment fee. But I also knew that if they worked hard, they could change their lives. In these cases, I have simply made a gift of the enrollment fee. I recommend you do this only in very particular circumstances. It has been my experience that often people do not value what they do not personally have a stake in. They don't put in the time or the effort to make their business work and often end up blaming you when it doesn't. Make sure, as best you can, that the recipient of such a gift is going to make the most of the opportunity.

If you have a prospect that is not able to join right away and you do not wish to cover the enrollment fee yourself, stay in touch with them while they are raising the necessary funds. Let them know that you are eager to work with them and will do all you can to help them get started.

Chapter 11

THERE'S NO GUARANTEE

Someone has asked me if I would guarantee that they would make money! As soon as I recovered from my initial disbelief that someone would ask such a thing, I remembered exactly what to say - NOPE.

How can I guarantee you will be successful? How can I guarantee that you will make money? That's like opening a restaurant and asking the chef for a guarantee that people will like the food. Or opening a retail shop and asking your vendors to guarantee that you'll have customers to buy their merchandise. How silly would that be?

You can't guarantee your team members will make a dime. You don't know their work habits. You have no idea how persistent they are. Are they serious about building a business or are they looking for a get-rich-quick scam? Are they trainable? Will they take suggestions from you and the rest of the team? Will they quit the first time they get a rejection? Do they understand that network marketing is a great way to start a business or are they afraid of being laughed at? Will they promise not to hound their friends and family and then quit when they get told no? Will they let you teach them how to generate real leads for their business and not settle for the first warm body through the door?

I can't answer any of those questions. Neither can you. Only they can. So they are the only ones who can guarantee that they will make any money. But you can guarantee them something. If they keep doing what they have been doing - what they know isn't working – then next year, 5 years from now, 10 years from now, they will be exactly where they are today. How's THAT for a guarantee?

Can You Tell Me How Much I Will Make?

I love it when prospective business partners ask me this question. I want to pull out my magic crystal ball and give them an answer. But honesty is really best in this situation - for two reasons. First, they don't expect it and so it will give you an opportunity to show them that you really are a professional with a legitimate business opportunity and you are not going to make promises that neither of you may be able to keep. Second, it shows them that the income they earn is largely dependent on what they do...or don't do.

I have hundreds of people on my team. Most of them are at least moderately successful. Some of them are not. I have team members who are millionaires. I have team members who are making $60K or more a year. I have team members who are only making an extra $1000 or so a month. And I have team members who haven't made a dime.

And I'll admit – some of the successful ones took me by surprise. And a couple that I really expected would do well are getting ready to quit.

What made the difference?

Effort. Listening to me and other upline leaders. Persistence.

Faith.

How much will they make? I don't know. You don't know. They could change their life. Or they could continue as they have all these years.

All I do know is if they don't do it, they are guaranteed to make exactly zero dollars.

How to Make Money With Network Marketing

Let's get two things straight right now. Starting a network marketing business involves a bit more than joining someone's downline and then sitting in your living room waiting for the money to start coming in (see "Top 10 Strategies for Becoming a Professional Network Marketer" in the appendix). However, if you have some discipline and can learn from those who really do make money in MLM, then you can make a decent living.

So what does it take to get started in network marketing? It's fairly simple. Choose your company. Try to choose one you are passionate about so you'll stick with it long enough to see some results. See "How do I know which Network Marketing Company is best?" and my list of "The Top 10 Network Marketing Companies" in the Appendix for suggestions.

Next, find a sponsor who will work with you. Attend some business presentations. Talk to those who are actually having success. Look for the leaders in the group. When you find someone you feel comfortable with, ask to join their team.

Now, learn all you can about your business and your products. What is the comp plan? How do the products work? How do you sign up new team members and customers? This knowledge is critical if you want to be successful.

The next step is to figure out a way to reach your potential downline members and customers. The best companies and sponsors will teach you how to do this, and you can also review the "20 marketing strategies to get you started" in the resource section of this book. There are tons of books, blogs, and newsletters available on this topic. I recommend several in the Resources chapter of this book.

Once you have identified your company, found a sponsor, learned all you can about your business, and created a marketing plan, then it's time to market your opportunity and products to your prospects. There are all kinds of ways to do this and what works for one may not work for you. The best way to learn about network marketing is to study what the experts have to say. If you can buy some of their products, great. If not, at least sign up for their mailing lists and newsletters. They are the "gurus" in this business and can teach you all you need to know. How do I know? Who do you think taught me?

This is just a brief outline of how to make money working a network marketing business. There simply isn't room to go in depth here. That's a whole book on its own. But if you will follow these basic steps and listen to the experts, you can make money in network marketing.

So - How Much Money Are You Making?

This is a frequent question. I am very careful how I answer it. I never quote an actual amount because it can cause problems. Never, EVER, answer that question unless you want to get this accusing phone call after someone fails to perform: "You told me I could make money!"

So when prospects ask me this question, I tell them I make enough to live on. So they get all excited and the next thing I get is an email or a phone call stating that they too have gotten involved in network marketing.

But I've actually had potential team members refuse to join because I wouldn't tell how much I'm making. In their opinion, this means I'm not making anything and don't want them to know the truth. Let's be real. It doesn't matter how much I make.

It's not about how much money you or I are making, it's about how much money your prospect is capable of making. The best answer is to be able to explain this and help them to understand that the only thing limiting their success is themselves.

If I make $10,000 a month does that mean you will? Of course not. And if I'm only making $10 a month, does that mean you will? No. I personally have sponsored several people who have gone far beyond what I'm making. And I have also sponsored several people who never made a dime.

What I'm making doesn't matter. What matters is how much you want to make.

Network marketing is a great opportunity. But like all opportunities, some people will take full advantage of it and some won't. If we all based our potential on the success of those around us, how many of us would ever accomplish anything?

The other supposed reason I won't tell prospects what I'm making is because we all know network marketing is a pyramid scheme and no one ever makes money in a pyramid scheme. All I can say to that one is read the chapter explaining the difference between a pyramid scheme and a legitimate network marketing opportunity. Then judge for yourself. If you still believe it's a pyramid, nothing I say will change your mind. In which case, it really doesn't matter how much I'm making because you're not joining MY team!

ACTION STEP:

- While you cannot tell how successful anyone will be or how much money they will make, you can explain how the comp plan works (see "Network Marketing Compensation Plans" in the Appendix). Study it so that you understand it completely and can explain it thoroughly and answer any questions.

- When someone asks for a guarantee, just say no. No guarantees. Prepare a list of the training and support that is available for all team members. Be able to explain that you can't guarantee that someone will be successful because it is dependent on how hard they are willing to work. Share the training and support available and explain that if they attend trainings and listen to conference calls, listen to their team leaders, and follow the advice and coaching of you and other leaders, it will be almost impossible for them not to be successful.

Chapter 12

HOW CAN I FIND THE TIME?

Soon after I started in business, I recruited two members to my team. Both were enthusiastic about the company and the products we offered. They attended trainings and business presentations. Only, one of them rarely brought a guest to the presentations. A year later, one of them was making more than I was. The other one quit. I'm sure you can guess which one. When I talked to them it was clear that both of them were pressed for time. They both worked full time and had jobs that required long hours. But one made the most of every spare minute. If he was waiting in line, he was on his phone with a prospect. Instead of watching television, he posted ads or held webinars. While running, he would listen to motivational tapes or training tapes. The other never seemed to find the time to share the business or the products with people. He contacted four or five people and when they didn't immediately sign up, he got discouraged and quit, blaming it on the fact that he didn't have time.

I often hear something like, "I have a full time job and an extremely busy life with 3 kids and my husband going back to school part time while still working his full time job. I want to get started in a network marketing business - although I'm not sure which one yet - but I don't think I have the time. How can I make it work?"

The answer is that you DO have the time. You just may need to make some adjustments to both your expectations and how you're spending your time. First, let's take a look at your expectations. If you think you are going to put in a couple of hours a week and yet be able to quit your job in 6 months, you need to adjust your expectations. That is just unrealistic. But if you and your husband are willing to continue to work your jobs and start your business part time, you can soon be bringing in a nice supplemental income while you continue to grow your business. In my experience, you will be more than able to build a nice supplemental income while working an hour or two each day.

If you have decided that a part-time business is fine while you grow, then the next thing you may need to adjust is how you spend your time. Get a calendar for the month. First, pencil in work schedules – both yours and your husband's. This is time that is already blocked and can't be used to grow your business. Next mark any other dates and times that are absolutely locked in - anything that can't be rescheduled or cancelled. Next, pick one day that is for you and your family. No work allowed. My day is Sunday. That's the day I very rarely do any type of work, but instead devote myself to church and family.

Now look at your calendar. Allowing for sleep of course, the remaining hours are the times you have available to work your business. Start scheduling yourself some "appointments." These don't have to be real appointments to meet with someone, but I have learned that if you write down a commitment to do something and schedule a time to do it, you are much more likely to actually follow through. So let's say we skip our favorite Monday night TV show and use that hour to call three prospects. Tuesday night perhaps your husband doesn't have class but he's on the computer doing homework anyway so let's schedule him to send an email to friends and family telling them about your new business. Wednesday, if you're a member of my team, is our training call, so let's schedule an hour for training. Thursday send a follow-up email or make a follow-up phone call to prospects who have already seen your initial presentation and haven't said yes or no yet. Friday perhaps you could write a blog post about residual income. Saturday schedule lunch with a prospect and do a one-on-one presentation.

My point is that in the beginning it's not so much the quantity of time spent as the consistency. Do a little something – ANYTHING - but do something every day to help your business grow. Read your company's materials, listen to training calls, watch DVDs, make a contact list of prospects, make a few phone calls, send some emails, mail a brochure, hold a business presentation. Write a blog post, place some advertising, host a webinar.

When starting your business, you do want to build a team as quickly as possible. Use that power of leverage to maximize your efforts. So spend some time on activities that build your team. An email to everyone in your mailing list announcing your new business is a great way to get the word out. Every new business announces their grand opening. Why wouldn't you do the same? Invite anyone who expresses some interest to a business presentation at your home. Hold a webinar or teleseminar about residual income or the concept of leverage. At the end you can give a link to your business website.

Not all recruits will be as determined as you are though, so until you have a high-functioning team, focus on personal activities that will help you meet your income goals.

This may sound a bit overwhelming but I assure you it can be done. The main thing is to be sure that you are setting goals. How will you know if you're working effectively if you don't know what you are aiming for? First, determine what your income goal is. How much money do you want to bring in each month? Be realistic. You are probably not going to make $10,000 your first month. Once you have a financial goal set, set a monthly sales goal and a monthly recruiting goal that will enable you to reach that income. Then determine what steps you will need to take to reach that goal and if it's feasible with the time you have available.

Let's plan your first month together. First, you will need to set a financial goal. In my company, it is entirely possible to make $1000 your first month. So let's use that as our goal.

Next, let's set a goal for recruits and customers. How many of each would it take to make $1000? Again, in my company it is possible to do so with only two recruits and 2-3 customers. So let's set that as our goal - 2 recruits and 2 customers. Now how do we get there?

Let's assume that we joined our company on Saturday. Since we are doing this part time while still working a job, that is likely the case.

First I have to be sure I am ready for business. So I am going to spend Saturday studying the comp plan and asking questions if necessary. If the company has a replicated website, I am going to be sure mine is available online and ready for traffic. If I don't, I am going to set up a blog so I have somewhere to send people who are interested in my business. I am also going to make sure my social media sites look professional since I am now an entrepreneur and I am also going to join any sites where I do not yet have a presence.

Sunday is family day. But I still might have a chance to share my new venture with church friends or family members!

Monday I am ready to hit it hard. First, I have to find some prospects. That means marketing. So my first efforts are going to be directed toward letting everyone I know that I am in business. So Monday after dinner, I am going to send an email to everyone in my contact list announcing the grand opening of my business.

Tuesday is Scout night (or soccer night or whatever the kids have going on) so while my husband takes the kids wherever they need to go, I'm going to check my email and see if I have any responses. If so, I am going to get them on a webinar or conference call or some other method of presenting the business opportunity. But what if I don't? That's okay. Do not get discouraged and do not quit. Since I don't have anyone to follow up with, I am going to write a blog post about one of our products and its benefits and include a link to a capture or sales page.

Wednesday, I check the email again and I do have a prospect. Since Wednesday is the company training call which I absolutely must be on, I ask my husband to follow up with our lead and to do a 3-way call with our upline sponsor while I attend the training.

Thursday, I follow up with the person we did the 3-way with the previous evening and oh my goodness, they want to enroll! So I spend the evening on the phone with my sponsor getting my new recruit set up and ready to go, while my husband does some social media posts about our nutritional supplements and how they have increased his energy level. He offers a sample to our social media friends.

Friday, I contact my new team member to ensure she is all set up and ready to go. And I share with her the same steps I am taking to get started (duplication, remember?). My husband, meanwhile, checks for email responses and then sees we have a couple of requests for more information on the supplements, which he promptly forwards.

And so, at the end of our first week, we already have one new team member and a couple of prospective customers. Every day do at least one thing to grow your business and you'll see that slowly but steadily, your team will grow, your income will grow and you WILL one day be able to take your part-time business to a full-time lifestyle. Good luck!

Tips and techniques:

When someone tells you they don't have the time, it's up to you to show them how they can build a successful business with the time they do have. Use the example above to teach your team members to block out a space of time every day, even if it's only an hour, to accomplish at least one task dedicated to building their business.

Additionally, ensure your team understands the importance of taking time to relax and recharge. Scheduling that one day to devote to family and self is just as important as the time scheduled for business activities.

Chapter 13

I'VE TRIED "THESE" BEFORE...

For the first time in a very long time, I actually walked away from a prospective team member. Willingly. Happily even. Why? Let me tell you the story!

I met up with a friend I hadn't seen in quite a while. Several years, in fact. She was still working for the same store I met her in years earlier when I worked there part time to make ends meet. She asked what I was doing and I told her. She expressed some interest so I gave her the DVD of the business presentation, not really expecting she would watch it or get back to me. Surprise! She did and called me the next day. She wanted more information. Usually all it takes for someone to make up their mind is to see the DVD, but I'm willing to give someone all the information they need. So next I got on a conference call with her and the number 2 guy in the entire company. She was very excited after that. When can we get together? She wanted to know. I told her I would stop by today, even though it is Sunday and I normally don't work much on Sunday.

I arrived at her house, paperwork in hand, thinking this is it. She was so gung-ho and excited, she was going to take this and run with it and truly change her life. I knocked on the door and she invited me in. We sat down, I took out the paperwork, asked her what name she would like her checks in, and heard, "I'm not sure about this. I've tried these before and none of them worked." I stopped dead. Which of "these" has she tried? The list was long - Mary Kay, Avon, Amway, Melaleuca, ACN...she's tried just about every business opportunity in existence and NONE of them have worked for her.

Now, I know that every opportunity is different. And I truly think my company is the best. But still - to have tried that many and not had any success at any of them? That's almost impossible. So I asked her why she didn't have any luck with her previous endeavors. The list of excuses was almost as long as the list of things she had tried and failed. No time, no money, didn't know anyone to show the products or business plan to, no support from her sponsor, no training...on and on she went. She blamed everyone and everything and took absolutely no responsibility for her failure.

I know most of these companies. They are all fine companies with good products and great people working them. I could understand if she had tried one or two with no luck. But according to her, she's been involved in 7 different businesses, none of them more than a year, and all of them a dismal failure.

I listened to her a little while longer telling me how most of "these" companies were just successful for only a select few. And then I said something I almost never say. "Perhaps you're right. Maybe you aren't ready for this yet. Why don't you think about it some more and call me when you are ready?"

I expect she never will be. Meanwhile, I'm just moving on. This is exactly the type of person you do not want. They are looking for a way to make a quick and easy dollar and when they discover there is no "easy" they will quit and blame you and your company. Sometimes they do this very vocally. The best thing you can do here is walk away. Granted, not all opportunities are created equal. What makes one company perfect for me may be exactly the thing that makes it completely wrong for you. But if someone has tried as many different companies as my friend, chances are it's not the companies, it's the prospect. Some people suffer from what I like to call Bright Shiny Object Syndrome. They want to make money but they don't really want to take the time to learn the skills and do the work necessary. And so they hop from one opportunity to another, looking for the magic system that will make them a ton of money with little or no effort on their part. They join a business, throw themselves into it for a little while. But then they discover that it takes more work and more time than they want to devote to it and gradually they stop working it at all. Then all of a sudden a new opportunity presents itself, promising all sorts of success, and once again they are off chasing their latest shiny object. There is nothing you can do for these people until and unless they finally realize that there is no magic bullet. Success takes work.

ACTION STEPS

Read "Top 10 Strategies for Becoming a Professional Network Marketer" in the appendix.

Chapter 14

THERE ARE SO MANY OPPORTUNITIES JUST LIKE THIS ONE...

The other side of the "I've tried these before" coin is the "These are all the same" objection. I hear this one every day. "I'm looking at another company that is just like yours." "There are so many opportunities just like this one." "Frankly, your business is a little expensive to get started in. There are lots of others that cost a lot less to join."

How do you compete with other companies all vying for the same reps? One thing you don't want to do is "negative advertising." You can find this sort of marketing all over the internet right now. Yes, it may work in the short term. But all you are likely to recruit using that method are the reps looking for the easiest way to make a fast dollar, and when they run into their first roadblock, they will quit. I hope you will never hear me badmouth another opportunity - and if you do, I hope you will remind me that it's never the right way to find prospective partners.

What do you do instead? Showcase the strengths of your own business. You joined for a reason. What was it? Do you have the best products on the market? Then discuss that. Show your prospects how easy it is to get sales and retain customers because of the quality of the products you offer.

Is your comp plan fabulous? Showcase that. I never go to a presentation without a printout that shows what the average rep at each level makes - and how long it takes on average to get there. It's a great prospecting tool.

Most of all, you want to highlight your team. The one thing that has made our company stand out for me is the team of people I work with. I've been involved with several network marketing companies. They all had great products and good comp plans. But the team leadership was lacking. That's not a reflection on the quality of the company. Many networkers just don't know how to build and then lead a team. That's why I always point out how our team works with you once you're on board with us. Once you compare, most prospects find that our training and commitment to your success make our team the best choice.

There are so many opportunities out there - but they are not just like yours. Highlight the things that make yours stand out from the crowd and don't resort to dragging down the others. You'll attract the kind of partners you want - positive people looking for the best opportunity for themselves and their families who are willing to do the work it takes to be a success. And that's the secret to building a strong business.

ACTION STEP:

What is it that attracted you to your business opportunity? What sets it apart from the others? What makes it the best? List the benefits of being part of your business and your team. Be prepared to share them whenever someone compares you to others.

Chapter 15

I NEED TO ASK MY SPOUSE

This is a very common objection if you are showing the business to only one half of a couple. Many network marketing experts tell you to respond with a statement such as "Do you have to ask your spouse before you make any decision?" I personally do not advocate trying to push for a commitment without the spouse. Believe me, spousal approval and support can be critical in having a successful team member! Remember the old adage "If Mama ain't happy, ain't nobody happy!" Nowhere is that more true than in network marketing.

In my case, I did it backwards. I joined my first network marketing company without consulting my husband. And it was not a good decision. Don't get me wrong. My husband is very supportive of my businesses – now. But at the time he was firmly convinced that all network marketing companies were nothing more than pyramid schemes. Oh sure, a few people did okay. But the average person simply lost their investment. The only way to get ahead in the world was to go to school, get a good job, work long hours, and save all you could until you retired.

But of course, I knew better. I had seen the light and it was bright and shiny! I was going to join this business and clean up. And so I did all the things my sponsor told me to do every day. And every day, my husband would ask me when I was going to stop playing and get a real job. If I asked him for help with the kids or housework, he reminded me that he had actually worked all day and was tired while I had simply played all day. Eventually we each became more and more resentful of the other one, until we were fighting almost every day.

Of course, we already know that my first foray into network marketing was a dismal failure. At the time I blamed it on the lack of support from my spouse. I felt embarrassed to show it to my family. I was failing and in the back of my mind was the nagging suspicion that perhaps my husband was right. These things didn't work. And yet I hated to admit that he had been right and I had been wrong and so I kept pushing, becoming more discouraged and resentful every day. Now I know that I failed, not because network marketing doesn't work, but because I am not suited for cold calling total strangers and trying to sell them on my business opportunity. And I have never been comfortable hounding my friends and family until they give in to pressure and join. It wasn't his fault at all. But the stress and the arguments and disagreements took their toll, not only on me but on the entire family. I would NEVER start a business without the full support of my husband. And I would never advocate pushing someone else to do it either.

The Solution

How do you address the spouse objection? First, find out if that is really the objection or if it's simply a delaying tactic. Ask your prospect a question such as, "You appear to like what I have shared with you. If your spouse were to agree and support your decision, would there be any other reason you couldn't join today?" Now they either have to say no, there isn't, or they must admit that there is indeed another factor in question.

If the prospect says yes he is ready to join if his spouse agrees, then get the business presentation in front of the spouse. Schedule an appointment as soon as possible to give your presentation to the spouse. Explain to your prospect that you want to give the presentation so that you can be available to answer any questions the spouse may have. Do not let your prospect try to explain the business to the spouse.

Do you remember the old game of telephone we used to play when we were kids? Everyone sat in a line or a circle. The first person would whisper something to the child next to him. Then that child would whisper the same thing to the next child, and so on, all the way down the line. The last child would repeat whatever was said out loud. And it usually sounded nothing like what was originally said.

Letting someone else try to explain your business is much like playing telephone. You will tell your prospect what you want him to know. And then you will hope he delivers that same message to his spouse. But chances are he will not get the presentation correct. He will not be able to clearly explain the compensation plan. He will claim you said things you never did. He could possibly even make misrepresentations that will get you in actual trouble. Why take the chance? If you want to deliver a presentation, then YOU deliver the presentation. Don't delegate your message.

In the event the spouse objection is actually a cover for a deeper concern, keep asking questions until you determine what that concern is and then address that specific objection.

Tips and Techniques:

Don't push anyone to sign up without their spouse's approval. But if they say they want to talk to their spouse, make sure that's the real objection. If it is, promptly schedule an appointment to show the presentation to the spouse. If you suspect it isn't, try to get to the heart of the true objection or fear, and address that.

Chapter 16

ALL MY FRIENDS TOLD ME THIS WILL NEVER WORK!

"Value your opinion. It's worth as much as theirs." – Unknown

The world is full of opinions. Everyone has them. The good news is that you are free to ignore them. Often, it is the best thing you can do. There is a long history of famous people that went against public opinion. Thankfully they did, because they went on to achieve great things.

Are you a Stephen King fan? I love his books. But if he had listened to the publishing companies we wouldn't have his extraordinary stories to enjoy. Because they rejected his first book. He almost listened to them and would have destroyed the manuscript. Fortunately, his wife had her own opinion!

How about Jay-Z? Everyone knows him. Either because they like his music or because they know he is married to Beyonce. He started his own record label. Why? Because it was the only way he could get a recording contract. No record label would sign him.

Do you need one more example? Okay. Have you seen any of these movies: Schindler's List, Jurassic Park, or Jaws? I'm sure you have seen at least one of them or some other movie directed by Steven Spielberg.

But when he applied to USC to study film, he was turned down. Not once but twice!

When I first started network marketing, my friends all told me the same thing. It will never work. I was with a different company then and they were right - it didn't work that well. Not because network marketing doesn't work or because that company wasn't a good one. It just wasn't the right one for me. I realize that now. But back then - when I failed - I thought they were right. This stuff doesn't work.

A few years later, desperate for extra money, I let myself get talked into trying network marketing again. A different company this time, with great products. And all my friends laughed and asked hadn't I learned my lesson the first time? But as a newly single mom, I really needed some extra income and so I tried again. This time I had more success. While I wasn't making millions, I was making enough to help make ends meet without having to get a part-time job. My friends saw my success and yet still insisted it wouldn't last. And besides, if it worked so well, how come I was only making a few hundred dollars a month? Despite their disbelief and lack of support, I remained with that particular company for many years, eventually building it so I was making a few thousand extra dollars each month. Not enough to support me, but it did pay for things like private school for my children, band and choir camps, and cars for them when they turned 16.

Fast forward to 2009. That's when I was introduced to my current company. It sounded like a great company with a good comp plan. Even my husband was impressed. We joined the first time we saw the business plan. And of course, all of our friends lined up to tell us the same thing we had heard before - these things never work. It didn't matter that they had watched me over the past years continue to make more and more money with network marketing. They still took great delight in telling us about all the people they knew who had tried "one of these" before and it didn't work. Well, I am delighted to tell them they're wrong. It does work - quite well.

I look back at all of this and I have to wonder - why? I see how they live. I know many of them aren't happy in their jobs, or are struggling to keep up with bills. I know they want the extras for their family that my family has. I can't begin to imagine what's holding them back. And those who ARE making decent money are often sacrificing time - time with family, time to worship, time to relax and recharge. Life is passing them by while they spend 50-60 hours a week in the office or factory. They slave away day after day making their employer wealthy while they receive a few dollars an hour in compensation.

Perhaps they are like the 5 Monkeys. You've never heard of them? Well I hadn't either until recently. But once I read of the 5 Monkeys experiment it seemed to explain these naysayers pretty well. To briefly summarize the experiment, 5 monkeys were put in a cage with a bunch of bananas hung out of reach and a ladder. Whenever a monkey would try to climb the ladder to reach the bananas, the experimenters would spray all of the monkeys in the cage with cold water. Eventually, whenever a monkey would try to climb the ladder, the other monkeys would pull him off the ladder and beat him. Then the experimenters removed monkeys from the cage one at a time and replaced them with new monkeys. Despite having never been sprayed, the new monkeys quickly learned that going up the ladder was not to be allowed and would beat any monkey who tried.

Now, think about your naysaying friends. Perhaps their parents or grandparents had tried for something that was just out of reach and had been "sprayed with cold water." Not only did they learn that it was wrong to reach beyond their place, they passed that lesson on to their offspring. So even though the naysayers may have never personally experienced the rejection, the lesson is now part of their mindset: don't reach beyond where you are.

So when you get this response from a prospect, I guess the real question you need to ask is this: Why are you taking financial advice from your friends? Unless you are a trained psychologist, you will probably never change the group mindset of the naysayers. If they see your lifestyle or that of your upline(if you're just starting), if you have shared the confidence and excitement you have in this business, and they still don't get it, they probably never will. You are not going to successfully recruit everyone around you. Don't waste your time on people with the naysayer mentality. Next!

TIPS AND TECHNIQUES:

- There is almost nothing your prospect can do to overcome the objections coming from their naysaying friends and family members, but you can help your prospect realize that the naysayers are drawing from their own inexperience and insecurity and that their opinion has no bearing on your prospect's ability to succeed. Remind your prospect of those people in the industry who are wildly successful, and even mention famous people who succeeded when others told them they would fail.
- Review "Top 10 Strategies for Becoming a Professional Network Marketer," found in the appendix of this book, with your prospect.

Chapter 17

UNDERSTANDING PERSONAL ATTRACTION

We've discussed the major objections typically encountered when presenting your network marketing business. They all sound like different concerns. Some prospects are concerned about their reputation. Some seem concerned about the legality of the business model. Others are wondering if they will make enough to be worth their time. And still others are so concerned about every aspect, they won't even take a look at your opportunity.

It's easy and convenient to think these are all separate concerns and to deal with them as individual concerns. But as I stated in the beginning of this book, they are all manifestations of the same problem – fear. And our fears are caused by our insecurities. Our mindset can often stop us before we ever even get started. But you can overcome your fears. Some people call this tool Positive Thinking. Some call it Positive Action or Personal Attraction. We will call it Attraction Marketing.

Let me start by admitting that when I first started reading about personal attraction and The Secret and the Attractor Factor, I was extremely skeptical. I mean really, who believes you can simply attract what you want in your life solely by making your intentions known and then waiting for it to come to you? Now I realize that there is much more to it than that. And I am here to tell you that there is some truth to it.

When I started in network marketing, I did all the things my upline told me. I held business presentations in my home, handed out DVDs and CDs that talked about the business opportunity. I bought leads and faithfully followed up with each and every one of them. I paid for referrals and handed out information and business cards at every networking event I could get to. And I made a grand total of $35.46 a month. That's when I decided I either needed to find a better way or quit.

ATTRACTION MARKETING IN ACTION

I started researching to find who actually was making real money - and I mean 6-figures or better - in this industry. And when I found them, I studied them. I read everything they wrote, went to hear them speak, attended any presentations they did. And I discovered two things - either they had a loyal following already that came into this business with them, or they had somehow managed to build a business without doing all the things my upline was telling me I had to do. I was determined to find out how these people were getting customers and business partners to join them without having to hunt down every warm body they crossed paths with. That's how I found Mike Dillard.

Mike is an industry legend. One day while researching online, I discovered his website. As I read through it, I realized he was proposing doing business exactly the way I envisioned it should be. I promptly purchased his "Magnetic Sponsoring" Course. When it arrived, I immediately dove in. And there I discovered the traits that make a good ATTRACTIVE leader. I started watching the leaders on our local teams to see which of these traits they possessed.

As I watched these people in action, I noticed they all had a few things in common, and these things literally attracted success. Their success was not the byproduct of wishful thinking, but the result of applying Attraction Marketing. Here are the similarities I noticed:

All of them were extremely self-confident. They didn't feel the least bit self-conscious about promoting their business opportunity and products.

They all had goals. They knew exactly what they wanted and they were all focused on getting it.

They had rules. And if you wanted to be part of their team, you followed the rules. I particularly remember one individual who made it clear that his time was valuable and if you wanted to work with him and his team then you needed to be available for training calls or workshops or whatever he felt was necessary – and if you weren't, he would simply ignore you from then on. Fortunately, I was able to work my way back into his good graces and I never made that mistake again!

They shared their knowledge. If you were lucky enough to be around them, they would teach you what they had learned. This made them valuable. Even if you weren't a member of their team, many of them would still share what they knew.

They were always upbeat, positive, and optimistic. To the point that at first, I found it slightly annoying. Who can be that cheerful all the time? I found out later that sometimes each of them felt a bit down, but they quickly talked themselves into a more positive frame of mind. And they taught me how to do that also.

They took care of themselves. They respected themselves and those around them. If we went out together, they were not the last ones to leave, having had more than their fair share of food and drinks. They made sure they left at a reasonable hour so they were well rested. They didn't abuse alcohol, or drugs, or food. Many of them had a regular exercise routine. They took care of their appearance so even if they weren't sporting the latest designer fashions, they were still neat, stylish, and professional-looking. Their cars were well maintained, their houses were well maintained, their yards were neat and nicely landscaped. They cared for, loved, and protected their families and their friends.

In contrast, I have to admit, I often felt embarrassed about promoting network marketing. I still pictured it as only quasi-legal and not a real business at all. I had goals - sort of. I knew I wanted to make more money. I didn't know exactly how much or how long I would take to get there. I accepted all the excuses my few team members kept giving me for why they weren't working on their businesses. Heck, I had used them myself to explain my own lack of success. I only passed on to my team the info I received from my upline - which wasn't much. And I surely didn't share it with others! Why help someone who was working for someone else? I will be the first to admit that some days, my house looked like a bomb went off inside, and my car always looked like it could use a trip to the car wash. My yard always looked like it needed a touch with the lawn mower and my few flowers were usually more dead than alive. I showed up for business presentations and meetings in jeans and t-shirts. And I had long ago alienated most of my friends and family by continually pushing them to join my business. No wonder I was having a hard time convincing others I had the secret to success!

Changing Your Mindset

Several years and much learning has passed. And now I know how these leaders attracted people and prosperity to them with ease. I do it. You can do it too. But first you are going to have to change the way you think about certain things. Ready?

Step 1. You must learn to have an abundance mentality. When you approach someone or something out of need, your desperation shows. That either gives the other person all the power, since they now know how needy you are, or it convinces them you are a phony. If you were doing all that well, why would you need them so badly?

Step 2. You have to learn to take criticism in stride. I still get emails and phone calls telling me I am a scam artist, or network marketing is just a get rich quick scheme or blaming me because they are not making any money. I know now that I am not responsible for these people and that until they take responsibility for themselves they will never be successful. I can't help them until they do and so their comments no longer offend me.

Step 3. You must learn to say no. I no longer accept every warm body that approaches me about joining my team. You must learn that you can't work with everybody and it doesn't matter.

Step 4. You must take care of those around you. Your family, your friends, your team, your community. What you send out, you get back many times over. I have a friend who sells cars very successfully. Every day he makes it a point to do something nice for one of his customers. He calls it "feeding the lot." You know what? His customers love him and are very loyal. And if they have a friend or family member who needs a car, guess who gets the referral? That's how I met him. He sold me my car based on a referral from someone else. Besides, there is nothing like "care" to gain long-term, loyal customers.

Step 5. You must take care of yourself. No more jeans and t-shirts for me unless I am just hanging around the house. My husband and I are remodeling our home so it's the house we always wanted. We both hate yard work, so we have hired someone to do it for us. I make sure I get enough rest, and I am working to reach a healthier weight. And the fast-food dinners have come to an end. I love to cook and my husband has discovered that healthy eating can taste good.

Step 6. You must learn to communicate with poise, authority, and confidence. If you don't know how, my good friend Felicia Slattery can help. She's amazing and will have you speaking like a professional speaker in no time. (You can find her contact information in the Resource section.)

Step 7. Realize that you will spend the rest of your life learning. There is no magic bullet or superbook or e-course that will teach you all you need to know. One of the things that will make you attractive to others is your perceived value to them. And in order to have value you must acquire knowledge and skills that you can share. So if you think I am going to tell you to buy this book or take this course and be done – guess again. I do recommend books or courses or programs that have helped me. But you will also have to do some learning on your own. And if you find something that works, I hope you will share it with me.

So what is the secret of attraction marketing? There is no secret. You already have everything you need. You just need to learn to perfect it and then to use it and then to share it. You can do it!

Conclusion

LET'S DO THIS!

Network marketing can help you transform your life. Do you have dreams? Do you have the persistence, perseverance, patience, and discipline to realize them? Yes? Then the power to change your life is in your hands.

I can't promise you it will be easy. In fact, I can guarantee you that in the beginning there will be days you want to quit. That's just the nature of starting a business – any business, not just network marketing. I can also promise though that if you don't give up, you will be successful.

I wrote this book to help you have the best possible chance at succeeding. You have as much right to succeed as anyone. You just need the right tools.

Objections come from fear. And fear can be overcome. You have the tools now to help your prospects move forward. But YOU may also experience fear. You are embarking on a new path. I am asking you to change the way you think and act. I am asking you to do things you may have never done before. Use the tools you have been given to quell your own internal objections. You have nothing to fear!

If you need some inspiration and encouragement, sign up for my newsletter at my website (http://www.melodieannwhiteley.com). The advice, tips, and encouragement we share will help you succeed no matter which company you are in.

I hope I have given you the courage to face those dreaded network marketing objections head on! The next time someone asks, "Is this one of those pyramid things?" you will know exactly what to say. So are you ready? Let's do this!

P.S. Remember that promise I made? That you would have access to me? Well, I do keep my word. If you purchased this book and want to connect with me, go to my website and contact me via email. Tell me you purchased the book, and that you are holding me to my promise. I'll send you my direct personal email. Just like I said I would!

Appendix

HOW DO I KNOW WHICH NETWORK MARKETING COMPANY IS BEST?

I get this question - and dozens of variations of it - almost every day. "How do I know your company is the best?" "How do I know it's not a scam?" "How can I convince people to join when I'm so new, I don't know anything about it myself?"

There are dozens of opportunities out there - some legit and some not. Many of them promise to make you rich beyond your wildest dreams - overnight, while you sleep, with no effort on your part. That's usually a dead giveaway that it's not a good choice. Those companies will lead you to the first stumbling block in network marketing disaster - failure to build a downline. People that get involved with these types of "opportunities" have the "get-rich-quick" mentality that makes them highly unlikely to commit to your team long-term. They will bail after the first few months of minimal income (my first check from one of these was a whopping 84 cents and I never made more than $20 dollars a month the entire time I was involved - which was before I learned the facts about network marketing). Or once they discover that in order to actually make "real" money you have to either invest some money of your own or actually put in some "real" work, they will be gone to the next flashy promise.

So the first sign of a good network marketing business is one that lets you know up front that money can be made - if you are willing to do the work. By the way, don't confuse a bad associate with a bad company.

Unfortunately, there are perfectly great companies misrepresented by associates who will promise you anything to get you on their team. Don't take the word of the person recruiting you unless you know and trust them. Check out the company for yourself and see what they actually promise.

Second, look at the compensation plan. Can you actually build a team and customer base big enough to make some money? How many levels down will you be paid commission on? Are there breakaways (a team member promotes to the same level as you or higher and leaves to start his own downline, taking everyone he has recruited so far with him). Do you have to buy products yourself or hit a certain quota to get paid? The first company I joined had great products and a stellar reputation. But you had to have a huge downline or tons of customers to make any money. Still not a problem except for one thing. You were not allowed to mention the company name in any promotional material until the prospect asked for more information. And you were not allowed to use any type of capture or squeeze pages to build a contact list. So how were you supposed to build your business? Door-to-door, in-home parties, and hounding everyone you knew. Plus you had to purchase a certain amount of product yourself each month to get a check. No thanks. I'd rather have a job. Lots less hassle!

Third, check out the support and training. Is there actual training? Do you have the phone numbers of your upline sponsor and perhaps his sponsor and maybe even two or three more people above him? Is there promotional material available - either free or at an affordable cost? Is your upline willing to assist you while you begin to build your customer base and downline?

Last, but most important, look at the product. All of the above is meaningless if you're selling a product that you don't believe in. That's what you want to focus on. Selling the product. If you focus on just building a downline, once you run out of friends and family to recruit, how are you going to continue to grow? Selling the product provides you with a ready-made list of prospects for your business. That's how I got involved many years ago with a company called Melaleuca. I loved the products and used them regularly. I STILL use them. So when my salesperson asked if I'd like to know more about the business opportunity, it was an easy decision. The product sales are where the money comes from. So unless you're planning to buy a whole bunch of whatever it is yourself, you'd better have some customers. The biggest downline in the world is useless if the company isn't making enough sales to pay you.

Now you know what to look for. The choice is yours. Simply look at the companies that interest you and run them through this checklist. Then choose the one that best meets your needs.

THE TOP 10 NETWORK MARKETING COMPANIES

Which network marketing companies are the best? That really depends on who you ask. We all have our favorites. Not every company is suited for everyone. But after years of working with several different companies, I have 10 that I think have the most potential for success. I am personally involved with a couple of these companies and can personally recommend them. My other choices were made after much research. If you are looking for a network marketing company, I'm sure you will find one here.

1. Ariix (www.ariix.com): Ariix is a health company offering some of the most high quality and cutting-edge wellness products on the market. There are plenty of health and wellness companies. But this is the first network marketing company I have ever seen that has a team member bill of rights. That makes them #1 in my list!

2. Melaleuca (www.melaleuca.com): For 27 years, Melaleuca has been leading the way in selling concentrated products and preserving nature's resources.

3. Isagenix (www.isagenix.com): Isagenix offers health and wellness product solutions for weight loss, energy and performance, and healthy aging. This three-tier approach practically guarantees you will always find a market for at least one of their products.

4. Amway (www.amway.com): One of the world's largest direct selling businesses. And the oldest. Amway has been in business for over 50 years, with nutritional products, bath and body products, beauty products and more. I attended my first Amway business presentation while I was in college!

5. USANA (www.usana.com): USANA Health Sciences is one of America's leading companies in the field of health and nutrition. The company has been in business for over 20 years and offers multiple ways to earn income.

6. NuSkin (www.nuskin.com): Founded in 1984, Nu Skin is a direct selling company that distributes more than 200 premium-quality anti-aging products in both the personal care and nutritional supplements categories.

7. Forever Living (www.foreverliving.com): Founded in 1978, Forever Living is a multi-billion dollar company, based in Scottsdale, Arizona, that manufactures and sells dozens of wellness and beauty products.

8. Herbalife (www.herbalife.com): Herbalife is a global nutrition company that has helped people pursue healthy, active lives since 1980. Their products are available exclusively through independent Distributors in more than 80 countries.

9. LegalShield (www.legalshield.com): As one of the first companies in the United States organized solely to design, underwrite and market legal expense plans to consumers, LegalShield has been in business for nearly 42 years and now provides legal services to over 1.4 million families across the U.S. and Canada.

10. ACN (www.acninc.com): ACN is the largest direct seller of telecommunications and essential services in the world. It has even been personally endorsed by Donald Trump.

NETWORK MARKETING COMPENSATION PLANS

One of the most important things to look at when choosing a network marketing opportunity is the compensation plan. Unfortunately it is also one of the most confusing.

While the compensation plan may not be the deciding factor when choosing which company to work with, it can contribute significantly to your success if you understand how it works – and to your failure if you don't.

There are several different types of compensation plans used in MLM today. One of the oldest is the Unilevel plan. This is also one of the easiest to understand since you are only allowed to sponsor one level on your team. In other words, everyone you sponsor is on your front line. This makes it easy to explain to prospects which may help in your recruiting efforts. However, if you are recruiting from your warm market (i.e. friends and family) it can make it difficult since you will be setting them up to compete against each other since they are all on the same level. If the opportunity you are considering uses this model for their compensation plan, be sure you are comfortable recruiting from your cold market in order to build a large frontline organization.

Another common compensation plan is the Stairstep Breakaway plan. In this plan, members of your team can advance up the ranks and when they reach a certain level, they are allowed to break away from your line and start an organization of their own. This allows them to earn larger commissions and so is a great incentive for them to work while they are still in your downline. However, while you normally would receive a smaller "override" commission from the breakaway organization, your overall commission can take a serious hit initially. But if you are comfortable in your ability to recruit and train new team members, this can be a great plan for building long-term residual income.

The Forced Matrix plan has a limited width and depth for which you will be compensated. For example, in a 3x3 matrix plan your frontline will consist of 3 team members and you will earn commissions only 3 levels deep. If you recruit a third person, they will automatically be placed into the downline of one of the first two. The Matrix plan can help you recruit since new team members can rely on this to help build their business while they gain experience. This plan also encourages leaders to assist their team in building their organizations once their own frontline is full. However, since it is very hard to explain and can give the appearance of the dreaded "pyramid scheme", it can make it make it equally difficult to recruit new team members.

Another, more recent compensation plan to arrive on the scene is called the Binary plan. As the name suggests, this is based on the number two. Therefore, you would be allowed to have a maximum of two team members in your frontline. Anyone you enrolled after that would automatically be placed under your existing frontline members. This encourages the team to work together since everyone benefits from building a strong downline. Another advantage is that most companies allow their members to start another downline (commonly called business centers in this plan) once they have reached a certain level with the first.

Many companies also offer additional incentives to their compensation plans, such as free trips and cars (think Mary Kay's Pink Cadillac).

TOP 10 STRATEGIES FOR BECOMING A PROFESSIONAL NETWORK MARKETER

Network marketing is becoming more popular as people try to supplement their income, or replace income from lost jobs. It's one business where almost anyone can be successful. But many people I know are still only doing it either part time in addition to their regular job, or they regard it as only temporary, until they find a new job. What does it take to cross that line from part-time networker to professional network marketer?

1. Know your business. You should be completely familiar with your company and its products, its compensation plan, what support is offered to new reps, and how to get new reps started in the business. If you don't understand it, you won't be able to explain it to potential customers or prospects. If you are new and still learning, make sure you know who to contact that can answer these questions for you.

2. Stay the course. I can't tell you how many fellow network marketers I know who are always chasing the next big thing. They don't stick with anything long enough to be successful at it. Do your research and pick the company that is best for you. There are many good ones. Once you have found the company that meets your needs, stay with it. Focus on this one business until you reach your goals.

3. 3. Learn to communicate effectively. Network marketing is a people business. If you can't communicate, you will never be successful. You can generate or purchase all the leads in the world, but if you can't convert them to customers or business partners,

it won't make a bit of difference. And to do that, you will have to talk to them. I don't know too many network marketers who have joined a company based solely on a web page, DVD, or recorded call. And while I have gotten a few customers from my website, most of them wanted to talk to someone before they made a purchase.

4. Know what you are marketing. When I started in the business, I was failing miserably. Then I discovered Mike Dillard and I learned one thing from him that has made all the difference. It's not about your company, or your comp plan, or your products. Sure, these things are all important. But the number one thing your prospects are buying is you! Become a person of value and learn to market that and you can join almost any company and your people will follow you.

5. Take action! No one is going to build your business for you. You will have to do something. I had a team member who continually complained because he wasn't making any money. He finally quit and then devoted quite a bit of time to convincing everyone that the business was a scam. And yet whenever we asked him how many people he had talked to, or how many presentations he had given, or how many ads he had placed, the answer was always the same - zero! If he had spent half the energy building his business that he spent trying to convince everyone it was a fraud, he'd be well on his way to financial independence by now.

6. Finish what you start. A few years ago I had the opportunity to meet Carrie Wilkerson. And she made a statement that has stuck with me ever since. Taking action is great but it's not enough. You have to take massive action to COMPLETION!

7. Target the right people. Please - do not hound your friends and family to join your business. They probably aren't interested. If

they are, they will let you know. Who do you want to look for? People who are already in the business but aren't having much success with the company they are in. People who are already successful network marketers. People who are actively looking for information on network marketing opportunities. These people already understand the business well enough to know that it is a good fit for them.

8. Learn to harness the power of the internet. The easiest way to find your target market is by learning to use the internet effectively. There are some great people who can teach you what you need to know - Ken McArthur, Diane Hochman, Brian Basilico, Heshie Segal and Rick Billings are five of my personal favorites.

9. Teach what you have learned. It's not enough for you to use these strategies. You have to lead your team in the same direction. Teach your front line reps what to do and then train them to teach their reps the same thing. Soon you will have an entire organization that is continually being trained to use the same strategies that are working for you.

10. Make a plan. Every business needs a plan, even a network marketing business. Set your goals and then use these strategies to build a plan to reach them. Decide today to become a professional network marketer and then do it!

RESOURCES

I have mentioned several people, books, blogs, and other tools throughout this book. Each of them has been invaluable to me. They will also be valuable resources for you. I have personally used and therefore am totally qualified to recommend them. Yes, I am an affiliate for some of these products. (Multiple streams of income! Gotta love that concept!) That means I will receive a commission if you purchase them. In the interest of fulfilling any legal obligations and because it is only fair that you have all the information, I will indicate my affiliate products by an asterisk (*).

PEOPLE

Starting your own business comes with its share of challenges. You will make plenty of mistakes along the way. One way to minimize the number of missteps is to find a good mentor or coach to help you. Not only are the people listed here experts in their field, they love sharing what that expertise with others.

Ken McArthur (www.kenmcarthur.com): Ken is an author, marketing expert, legendary creator of Impact, and the resident expert in forming partnerships and collaborations. I met Ken when he became one of my clients while I was working as a site selection specialist. Ken taught me the most valuable lesson of all - I don't have to do this alone. There are lots of experts available who are more than willing to share their knowledge, time, contacts, and advice with me – and with you.

Felicia Slattery(www.feliciaslattery.com):I met Felicia many years ago on the social networking site, Ryze, and came to admire and respect her long before I had the opportunity to meet her in person. Felicia taught me the value of being able to communicate effectively in any format. And then she taught me how to do that. If you are afraid to speak in public, or if your communication skills are somewhat lacking, I highly recommend you check out her products and services.

ProBlogger (Darren Rowse)(www.problogger.net): I discovered ProBlogger through a teleseminar that mentioned a man

(ProBlogger) that was bringing in a six-figure income simply from blogging. I immediately went to his site and through his teaching, entered the world of blogging for myself. I wasn't interested so much in blogging for money. But I was intrigued by the possibility of using blogging to build my network marketing business. And it worked!

Carrie Wilkerson (http://carriewilkerson.com): I had only known of The Barefoot Exec for a few months when I met her in person. But she made a powerful impression on me with her reminder to focus and that nothing gets accomplished without massive action TO COMPLETION!

BOOKS

Books are an invaluable resource when it comes to learning how to build your business. There are some great books on network marketing available. These are my top 10 picks. I have gleaned something of value from each of them. I hope you find them just as useful.

1. *The Business of the 21st Century* - Robert Kiyosaki: When Robert Kiyosaki writes, I read. He never fails to deliver. This book is no exception. It provides a great overview of the network marketing concept and its advantages and challenges. It has been a great asset when explaining network marketing to my prospects.

2. *Be a Network Marketing Superstar:* The One Book You Need To Make More Money Than You Ever Thought Possible - Mary Christensen: More of a workbook than most other books, which guides you through 26 steps to becoming successful in network marketing. I love this book!

3. *Your First Year in Network Marketing:* Overcome Your Fears,

Experience Success, and Achieve Your Dreams! - Mark Yarnell: Strategies for overcoming those obstacles we all experience in our first step into network marketing.

4. **Beach Money:** Creating Your Dream Life Through Network Marketing - Jordan Adler: This book is filled with inspiring stories about Jordan's own climb to success. Each story contains tips and ideas to help you build your network marketing business.

5. **How to Build a Multi-Level Money Machine:** The Science of Network Marketing - Randy Gage: The title says it all. No hype. No fluff. Just all the information needed to build a successful network marketing business.

6. **Do Due Diligence:** Cutting Through the Crap in Network Marketing - Greg Hartman: The resource list and due diligence questions make this book well worth reading.

7. *The Greatest Networker in the World* - **John Milton Fogg:** This book tells the story of a young, discouraged network marketer who is about to quit the business - until he meets the greatest networker in the world.

8. *101 Ways to Build a Successful Network Marketing Business* – Andrew Griffiths and Wayne Toms: Practical tips on how to succeed in network marketing.

9. **Being the Best You Can Be in MLM:** How to Train Your Way to the Top in Multi-Level/Network Marketing - John Kalench: Although an older book, there is still a wealth of relevant information in this book. Before his death in 2000, John Kalench was an extremely successful network marketer. In this book, he trains you just as he trained his own downline.

10. ***Dare to Dream and Work to Win:*** Understanding Dollars and Sense of Success in Network Marketing - Dr. Tom Barrett: Another older book but filled with practical information and tips that are easy to put into practice in your own business.

BUSINESS BUILDING TOOLS

If you are new to network marketing, you have one question on your mind. How do I build my team? If you have been in network marketing for years, you have one question on your mind. How do I continue to build my team now that I've exhausted all my friends and family contacts? Here are some great resources that I have personally used to build my own downline – WITHOUT having to recruit friends or family!

1. Site Build It!* (http://www.sitesell.com/Melodieann.html) –If you are going to do this business right, you will want to build your own website whenever possible. But why build a site that gets no traffic? Or put yourself at the mercy of someone else having control of your vision? Or add one more canned site to the hundreds of thousands already out there? Build your own business with Site Build It. You know if I can do it, ANYONE can do it!6.

2. Go Daddy (http://www.godaddy.com) You will definitely want a unique domain name of your own – even if you are forced to use a canned company website. You can still use your own domain to set yourself apart from the crowd and redirect it back to the company website. Which means you will need a great domain name registrar. Go Daddy is my personal favorite and the one I use to register my domains that are not hosted through SBI! They are the world's largest domain name registrar.

3. Free Conference Call.com (http://www.freeconferencecall.com) –

You will want to host teleseminars or training and recruiting calls. You will need a reliable, cost-effective, reservation-less and easy to use audio conferencing service. My team is spread all over the country. Free Conference Call.com helps me connect personally with them as a group.

4. Ezine Articles (http://ezinearticles.com) - A great way to drive traffic to your site is by publishing articles about network marketing. It establishes you as the expert and the person everyone wants to do business with. And Ezine Articles is the place to do it.

5. AWeber* (http://www.aweber.com) – Once you have a website and have used some of the methods and resources mentioned to drive traffic to it, you will need a way to follow up even when you are sleeping. That means you will need an autoresponder. And AWeber is the best.

6. The Network Marketing Magazine.com (http://thenetworkmarketingmag.com) – The Largest network marketing community in the world. Articles by respected network marketing experts. Business building and training resources. And the ability to meet and connect with other network marketers.

7. My Lead System Pro* (http://mwhiteley.bizbuildermastery.net/) - All of the tools and training you need to build lifelong residual income and all in one place.

20 WAYS TO MARKET YOUR BUSIBESS

If you need some inspiration to get you started on a marketing campaign, here are 20 ideas that I have used successfully:

1. Start an e-mail marketing campaign
2. Post client testimonials about your products on your website
3. Sponsor a charity event or local sports team
4. Host a free teleconference or webinar for your target market
5. Comment on blog posts
6. Host a giveaway on your website or blog
7. Start writing and submitting articles online (check out EzineArticles.com)
8. Offer incentives for referrals
9. Design a sales page for your latest product
10. Create an elevator pitch
11. Use your email signature to promote your business
12. Develop a pay-per-click campaign
13. Create a Facebook page
14. Attend a live event
15. Sign up for the Help a Reporter Out (HARO) e-mail list (I just discovered this and I love it!)
16. Run a contest and give away a free sample of your product
17. Write and submit a press release
18. Start a referral program
19. Launch a social media marketing campaign
20. Offer to speak at meetings and events

NETWORK MARKETING TERMS

Some of the terms used in network marketing can be confusing to new team members. Here's a short glossary of some of the more common ones.

Autoresponder: A program such as Aweber that responds to an e-mail or other inquiry without human intervention.

Business Builder: A team member who is actively gathering customers and building his own team.

Circle of Influence: Friends and family. People who are close to you and considered part of your warm market. People who might be easily influenced by you because of your reputation.

Depth: The number of levels in your Network Marketing organization.

Downline: The people recruited as distributors into a network marketing company.

Duplicatability: The extent to which a Network Marketing opportunity can be easily understood and implemented by new team members.

Renewal Fee: A yearly fee paid to a Network Marketing company in order to maintain your status as a distributor.

Saturation: The theoretical point at which a network marketing company runs out of potential customers and recruits.

Sponsor: A distributor in a Network Marketing company who recruits and trains another distributor.

Three-way or Three-way call: A recruiting call between a new recruit, his sponsor, and a new prospect. When a new recruit needs has a new prospect, he will three-way his sponsor or another experienced upline member into the call. The sponsor will do the business presentation and the recruit listens and learns.

Upline: All of the people above you in a network marketing organization

www.ingramcontent.com/pod-product-compliance
Lightning Source LLC
LaVergne TN
LVHW011729060526
838200LV00051B/3088